A Sociological Yearbook of Religion in Britain

[signature] 1973.

1968

A Sociological Yearbook of Religion in Britain

Edited by David Martin

SCM PRESS LTD

This book has been produced in co-operation with
Socio-Religious Research Services

S B N 334 01547 2

First published 1968
by SCM Press Ltd
56 Bloomsbury Street London WC1

© *SCM Press Ltd 1968*

Printed in Great Britain by
Billing & Sons Limited
Guildford and London

CONTENTS

THE CONTRIBUTORS

D. A. MARTIN Reader in Sociology, London School of Economics and Political Science, University of London

DONALD R. ROBERTSON Sociologist, 1341 Verdugo Boulevard, La Canada, California 91011

KENNETH THOMPSON Assistant Professor in Sociology, Rutgers University, New Jersey

JOHN GAY Assistant Curate, St James's, Sussex Gardens, London W 2

W. S. F. PICKERING Anglican Priest. Senior Lecturer in Sociology, Southlands College of Education, Wimbledon

J. A. JACKSON Senior Lecturer in Sociology, University of East Anglia

R. G. JOBLING Lecturer in Sociology, University of East Anglia

ERIC CARLTON Baptist Minister. Senior Lecturer in Sociology, Constantine College of Technology, Middlesbrough

MICHAEL DANIEL Anglican Priest. Lecturer in Sociology, Southlands College of Education, Wimbledon

F. T. PAGDEN Methodist Minister, 225 Stanks Drive, Whinmoor, Leeds 14

A. E. C. W. SPENCER Sometime Director, Newman Demographic Survey. Lecturer, Cavendish Square College, London W 1

BERNICE MARTIN Lecturer in Sociology, Bedford College, University of London

INTRODUCTION

THIS book appears as a response to an initiative coming from a group which was formed about three years ago to promote socio-religious studies, and which then comprised myself, Leslie Paul and Anthony Spencer. Anthony Spencer in particular conceived of a 'Bulletin' designed to tap the growing amount of British work in the field of the sociology of religion.

A growth of interest in the sociological analysis of religion has certainly been evident. Churches ask for the aid of sociologists and churchmen occasionally talk almost as if sociology could play a messianic role. And no doubt there are some clergy who find in it some alternative to the disheartenment of their professional experience. On the other side the formation of a religion section of the British Sociological Association and the meetings of the Religion and Society Dining Group show the growth of interest among sociologists. I hope that this volume and subsequent volumes can act as a vehicle for the work of those who are associated with these new initiatives.

Of course, whether or not future volumes appear depends on the response to the present venture. All publishing works by faith and not by sight and I am very grateful for the faith of the SCM Press. I would also like to show faith and speak about the future. The present volume is obviously eclectic, ranging from narrow concerns to broad ones and including varied material on the role of the professional clergyman, the geography of religion, the ecclesiastical bureaucracy, small cults and so on. Maybe it will be possible in future volumes to choose subjects more thematically. Next time, for example, we hope to consider the religious minorities of Britain, in particular groups like the Sikhs, Muslims, Cypriots and so on who now together form about 4% of religious adherence in this country (but excluding the Christian sects). There is also the possibility of analysing certain responses of African cultures to British religion. In other words, the religious aspects of culture contact form a focus in the plans for a second volume.

These intentions for the future may suggest an exclusive concern with empirical material based on the British scene. This will not be the case: there ought to be room for the occasional theoretical article and work on other cultures. But there are already a number of publications which carry theoretical articles as well as material ranging widely from Spiritualism in Sao Paolo to the Soka Gokkai in Japan. I am thinking in particular of *Social Compass*, the *International Yearbook for the Sociology of Religion*, the *Archives de Sociologie des Religions*, *Sociologia Religiosa* and the *Journal for the Scientific Study of Religion*. These I think are the proper avenues for reappraisals of functionalism, comments on the theoretical implications of Russian sects, reviews of recent work on Melanesian cargo cults, and so on. This yearbook will serve a useful enough purpose if it tries to collect, analyse and set within some broader framework the characteristic religious phenomena found in the British family of nations and in particular the United Kingdom itself.

DAVID MARTIN
*The London School of Economics
and Political Science*

1 The Relationship of Church and Class in Scotland

Donald R. Robertson

A SUCCESSFUL surveyor in his mid-thirties sits in the modest comfort of his suburban 'bungalow' and offers this compendium of thoughts on the church and religion.

Yes, I go to church quite regularly; it's always been a part of my life. It's the way I worship God, and I certainly want my children to have the benefit of training in church. But I would have to say honestly that I don't find the church services very enthralling most of the time – in fact, they border on being dull and dreary. In one manner or another, though, I feel it's good for people to have religious beliefs. Perhaps it doesn't matter so much what particular beliefs they hold and how they practise them. After all, there are, no doubt, many roads to God. However, I personally feel that the Christian Church still has an important part to play today: but it needs to come into the modern world, to get away from some of the formality and to be of more direct help to people. As things are going now, I'd have to say that the Church is fading rapidly.

Less than a mile distant, a middle-aged factory worker relaxes in the small lounge of his 'council' home and provides these observations.

No, I don't go to Church. It's been many years since I even entered a Church door. I suppose the main reason is that I feel I'm just as good a person without going. Besides, from what I remember of Church, it's all pretty boring, the minister droning on, the slow, sad hymns and all that. Now, don't misunderstand me: I'm not against the Church. I believe in God and in Christ, personally. Religious belief is a good thing; and for those who want it, going to church is all right too. But you don't have to put on fancy clothes every Sunday in order to be a good person. And I'll tell you what the Church needs most – that's to get a lot closer to the people. Ministers seem to be from a different world: they don't know what is happening today. Anyway, the only people who always go to church are middle-class women who think they have to go to be 'in' socially. As it stands now, the Church is rapidly losing ground.

Here we have, in the mouths of two stereotyped, hypothetical individuals, an epitome of prevalent practices and attitudes toward the church and religion in urban Scotland. Though representing two distinct social class groups and contrasting diametrically in overt religious practice, these contrived 'representatives' clearly share several common conceptions of the contemporary Church.

These epitomizations grew out of a study of 'relationship' to the Church of a number of middle-class and working-class men in Edinburgh. My purpose in this paper is to select and highlight some of the conclusions which emerge from this comparative study which I conducted in 1965 as a part of the preparation for a doctoral thesis in Sociology. The empirical investigation which served as the basis of the thesis (supported by two other surveys) consisted of a series of interviews 'in depth' with ninety-two men in the small Prestonfield district on the outskirts of Edinburgh. The study, in effect, probed a two-class 'microcosm' of urban Scotland. With this in mind, the title of the present paper is obviously somewhat pretentious and hyperbolic.

The sample of working-class men were, in the main, residentially situated within a pre-war 'council estate' that formed the central core of the Prestonfield Parish. Middle-class respondents were drawn from private bungalows and owner-occupied 'flats' surrounding the council estate, but within the same, geographically distinct, church parish. The working-class and middle-class groups were of approximately equal size in accordance with the study's methodological strategy (important in the facilitation of statistical comparisons). All of the men were interviewed within their own homes, with maximum rapport established and with the conversations tape-recorded. They were questioned concerning a wide range of class-linked and church-linked experiences and attitudes.

In this paper, I shall of necessity refrain from presenting the large body of statistical material which specifies various measures of class and church-relationship. Instead, some major conclusions will be extracted by way of explanation and interpretation of the 'findings'.

To begin, the question may be posed: What is the study's 'frame of reference'? What particular information was desired with regard to the intersection of these two institutional systems in Scotland, the stratification system and the religious system? Essentially, it was assumed that Edinburgh residents would reflect in their life experiences the general disparity between working-class and middle-class rates of church participation that have been empirically substantiated in a number of western industrialized societies. In brief compass, that general pattern is a substantially stronger support of established religious bodies by middle classes than by manual working classes.

Given this basic expectation – which received further confirmation in this Edinburgh survey – the prevailing purpose of the study was initially exploratory. The *raison d'etre* of the investigation was the hope of discovering interpretative linkages between class position and dimensions of relationship to the Church. The motivating desire was to ferret out, if possible, links of causal chains connecting stratification and institutional religion. Thus, the overriding question asked by this study, then, was not the question: 'What are the class-linked patterns of Church involvement?' but rather the question: '*Why* does the relatively greater abstention of working classes from overt religious practice so consistently obtain?' The exploration was, therefore, directed in search of 'explanatory' insights rather than to purposes of 'description' *per se*.

In addition to data serving to differentiate working-class and middle-class Church practices and attitudes, the study also reveals a number of interesting over-all profiles of attitudes toward the Church which appear to be shared by men whose socio-economic status varied widely. In the present summary article, attention will be given to these important points held in common – the apparent 'images' of religion in general and Church (primarily Church of Scotland) in particular. A backdrop to these prevailing conceptions is, of course, the widely noted decline of religious fervour in the present century and the increasing secularization of many aspects of life. Numerous churchmen, from their own perspectives, have deplored these trends.

In order to pursue this exploratory purpose, the survey first considered many facets of social class position. A basic division of interviewees into 'working-class' and 'middle-class' groups was made along the familiar 'manual' and 'non-manual' lines.[1] Obviously, this categorization was informed by the occupational positions of the respondents. In addition to occupational information a number of class-related variables – e.g. class-consciousness, political behavior, styles of life – were explored in order to test the empirical viability of the manual non-manual demarcation. In fact, these categories were vindicated, proving to be, as anticipated, more than mere statistical aggregates devised by the investigator. The manual 'working-class' groups and the non-manual 'middle-class' group were consistently and predictably distinct on virtually all measures, testifying to a considerable strength of class ties and countering the popular notion that class lines have become blurred and without significance in the era of post-war 'affluence'.

Though I cannot delve more deeply into this preliminary pursuit in this paper, it should be noted at the outset. Before attempting to determine the 'effects' of class membership in any area of experience, the strength and the meaning of class membership should be established; the 'independent variable' should be demonstrated to be valid and relevant – not an empirical artefact. There are, to be sure, many fascinating signs that the militancy and rancour of former class relationships have largely subsided, and that the securities of the welfare state have relegated to past history the worst catalogue of 'proletarian' misery and deprivation. None the less, the data of this study led unmistakably to a rejection of the notion of working-class 'embourgeoisement' – the upgrading of portions of the manual class into middle-class ranks. Class divisions appeared to be of overarching importance in determination of life styles, perspectives and identifications.

Turning now to the strategy of relating class position to the panorama of dispositions and practices connected with the Church, it may be first asserted that my purpose was one of separating the total idea of 'relationship to the Church' into its parts. Relationship to the Church is not a uni-dimentional phenomenon which is exhaustively depicted by such descriptions as 'goes to church' or 'does not go to church'. My operational assumption is that a person's church relationship may be along various lines, covert as well as overt. Measures of overt paticipation in the formal programme of the Church are certainly fundamental but they reveal only part of the 'story '– only a single 'dimension' of church relationship. One's 'attitudinal' posture may be equally germane: elements of perception of the Church's leadership, of her value to the individual and the community, opinions of church services and edifices and programmes, commitment (or lack of it) to norms and doctrines presented by the Church, etc. – all of these ought to be taken into account in the interest of a full appraisal of where the individual stands *vis à vis* the Church. So, the over-all purpose of this analytical or 'dimensional' approach is to get beneath the gross facts of class disparities in membership and attendance in church, and to try to ascertain some of the forces operating to produce the prevailing configuration.

On the whole, sociological investigations of religious behaviour have been confined to measurement of religious involvement in terms of overt church participation. Perhaps the most fruitful precursor of a multi-dimensional approach was Ernest Troeltsch's brilliant distinction between 'church-type' and 'sect-type' religious organizations.[2] In his classic work, Troeltsch demonstrated by a survey of organizational types in the history of the Christian Church that lower-status persons have often formed 'other-worldly', ascetic, emotionally satisfying sectarian bodies which provided personal belonging and meaning in a context of worldly deprivation. On the other hand, higher-status persons, who have a significant stake in the institutional scheme of society, have usually felt at home in highly formalized, rather ethically undemanding, 'church'-type organizations which are well accommodated to the values and forms of the *status quo*.

Recently, this seminal conceptualization has been employed by Nicholas Demerath in an American study.[3] He takes the distinction as the basis of his discussion of different *kinds* of participation by various status groups within the same religious organizations. This represents a divergence from the conventional church/sect distinction *between* religious organization, directly following the lead of Troeltsch. Demerath discovered, in accordance with his hypothesis, a more 'sect-like' propensity in the church-related religious practice of lower-status persons, and contrariwise, a more 'church-like' propensity among higher-status groups. The exposition of this 'typology' is a step forward in present-day sociology of religion, and it proves relevant to the explanations of certain findings in the Edinburgh study, as I shall later suggest.

More comprehensive in nature is a 'dimensional' paradigm of religiosity enunciated by Charles Glock.[4] He asserts:

A first and obvious requirement if religious commitment is to be comprehensively assessed is to establish the different ways in which individuals can be religious. With some few exceptions past research has curiously avoided this fundamental question. Investigators have tended to focus upon one or another of the diverse manifestations of religiosity and to ignore all others.[5]

Glock proposes that there are several distinct dimensions of religious experience that should be systematically separated for analysis: 'experiential' (emotional and perceptual content); 'ideological' (belief system adhered to); 'ritualistic' (all practices of religion – behavioural aspect); 'intellectual' (religious cognition and grasp of religious information); and 'consequential' (the effects of religious experience upon other, 'secular', areas of life). One of the implications of such a 'model' is that individual religious experience may be strong within some dimensions and weak within others. A person who avows he will 'never darken the door of the church' may, in some respects (such as adherence to a doctrinal system and practice of personal prayer) be a highly religious individual.

Developments in the progressively more analytical approach to variations in religious commitment and church commitment are illustrated by the foregoing references. In the Edinburgh investigation a somewhat different and condensed 'dimensional' distinction seemed warranted. So, the primary terminological distinction suggested is between church 'involvement' and 'church attachment'. The former refers to overt participation; the latter describes the wider set of dispositions toward the Church – doctrinal commitments, evaluations, etc. Viewed in a slightly different way, involvement refers to the 'behavioural' aspect of church relationship; attachment denotes the broad 'attitudinal' dimension. This central distinction allows for comparisons between patterns of direct participation and a wide array of attachments or 'attitudes' toward the Church and toward the religious values the Church represents. An underlying hypothesis was that these comparisons would be of major value in explaining and interpreting the notable class differences in church involvement. We shall see that this expectation is only tenuously confirmed.

However, before focusing attention upon the wide and revealing range of attitudes toward the Church, let us examine a small proportion of the available documentary evidence regarding rates of church involvement in Scotland in comparison with other western societies. Such a review will provide the reader with a notion of the wider context of church-class relationships in which the present investigation is situated.

It has been estimated, first of all, from available data that the average Sunday morning attendance in all Scottish churches encompasses about 26% of the adult population.[6] An array of surveys of varying scientific quality suggests that the average church attendance in England is about half the Scottish rate, or approximately 13% of the adult population.[7] By contrast, one western society of mainly Protestant character, the United States, has experienced a notable post-war 'revival' in church involvement. By 1962 the average weekly attendance had risen to nearly half (46%) of the adult population.[8] Whether the apparent upsurge of institutional religiosity in the US is merely an anomaly in the prevailing religious decline in the West, or is the augury of a pattern to be followed, in turn, by British and Continental societies, is, at present, problematic.

Class-linked variations in rates of church involvement have often been described in terms of the Church's failure to attract and 'hold' the working classes. For instance, with particular reference to England, Wickham has said: 'The extent of working-class estrangement is still insufficiently realized inside the churches, partly because the churches do not ask embarrassing sociological questions, and also, perhaps, because we have grown accustomed to the situation.'[9] Thompson, in his study of four Birmingham parishes, found similar class connotations and suggested that 'the congregations reflected rather than reconciled social divisions'.[10] Both national and local surveys in England have confirmed statistically the class disparities in church participation.[11]

In post-war France a considerable body of literature emanating from sociologically oriented Jesuits has indicated that the urban working classes are not only unengaged in church activities, but are often intractably hostile to the Church. Michonneau, on the basis of a Paris study, speaks of the French working class as a 'pagan proletariat'.[12] Emile Pin concluded from his Lyons investigation that:

Urban Catholicism appears remote, theoretical, impersonal and ineffectual. We might say that it is involved in all those aspects of urban life which are beyond the intellectual and practical grasp of the proletarian.[13]

Indeed, Isambert, who has gathered evidence from a number of European societies is led to discuss the possible use of the term 'sociological law' to describe this class-church configuration, so uniformly is the pattern found.[14]

Even in the United States, where a variegated denominational structure encompasses numerous lower-status 'sectarian' groups, there is evidence of significantly lower rates of working-class than middle-class church involvement.[15] Winter suggests that social distance has created in America a definite 'cleavage between old-line Protestantism and the working class. . . '[16]

To move rapidly back from the telescopic to the microscopic, the Prestonfield findings are consistent with the prevailing profile of church involvement disparities by class. They show 44% of the middle-class respondents describing themselves as attending church at least once a month, while only 17% of the working-class men indicated a similar frequency of attendance.

With this larger panorama in view, we appoach the central focus of the present paper, the range of attitudinal perspectives which indicate varying degrees and types of 'attachment' to the contemporary Church. Under the 'attitudinal' rubric a number of constituents of church attachment were examined: religious 'profession', doctrinal commitments, evaluations of the Church and of religious belief, and opinions regarding key representations of the Church (specifically, ministers, church-goers and church services).

Perhaps the biggest surprise of this investigation was *the limited degree to which different class rates of church involvement are correlated with variations in the measures of attachment*. In other words, the relatively greater abstention of working-class men from institutional religion seems to be only very partially explicable in terms of their perceptions, perspectives and evaluations of the Church in comparison with those of middle-class men. On the whole, members of both classes reveal strikingly similar patterns of attitudes. Indeed, much of the following material pertains to revelations of the general attitude profiles toward the Church common to both class groups in present-day urban Scotland. I shall also elucidate certain key 'clues' to the disparities in participation between the class groups which emerge from the findings of the study.

At this point, the stereotyped verbalizations with which the paper began to come to the fore again. The tone of casualness and tolerance regarding religious matters evidenced in the words of both working-class and middle-class spokesmen is suggested by responses to a number of questions put to the men in the Prestonfield survey. One measure of religious interest, for instance, is the frequency with which persons engage in personal discussions of religious questions. While middle-class men did indicate speaking with friends or family members about religion somewhat more often than do working-class men, the overall findings, for interviewees from both classes, showed a high degree of reticence about religion in their day-to-day affairs. Overall, 56% of the respondents said they *never* discussed religion; this fact, I think, stands out most strikingly. Many of the remainder suggested that religious discussions were rather infrequent events.

Respondents were also asked to explain (by selecting from a list of alternative replies) the reasons for their patterns of church attendance or non-attendance. Since about two-thirds of the total sample reported personal attendance at church very infrequently, seldom or never, the rationale for this non-involvement is quite germane. Interestingly (and class variations were negligible) about 30% explained their non-participation in terms of direct criticism of the

Church in some respect. Most of the remainder suggested some variation of the 'pure disinterest' theme: 'I can be just as good a person without going;' 'I don't have time to go;' 'I don't get anything from it;' and the like. Only a minuscule 5% of the men announced a position of disbelief in the Church or religion.

To wax more subjective in interpreting the tenor of explanations for church abstention, I detected a diffuse disaffection with the Church not usually associated with a particular consciousness of reason. Similarly, Thompson describes a Birmingham factory foreman whose former church activism had been dissipated as showing '. . . a sense of bewilderment at his own defection'.[17] This massive disinterest in what the Church has to offer cannot be understood in terms of conscious doctrinal rejection of the Church such as a disbelief in God. Even the few who opted for the 'disbelief' alternative did so more in the nature of puzzlement and provisional agnosticism than in the form of militant opposition to the Church's system of doctrines. Indeed, the Church has not apparently been rejected forthrightly even by those who ignore her. It is a lack of ability to attract, rather than a marked tendency to repel, that appears to restrict the Church's contact with large segments of the community, especially within the working class.

Further insight into the prevailing images of religion are obtained from interviewees' descriptions of 'what a Christian is' and their opinions of 'religious belief'. The majority defined 'a Christian' in terms of commendable character traits, or simply 'being good', rather than in doctrinal terms. The appellation 'Christian' seems to have been divorced from specific connotations of religious zeal or commitment and to have become a modestly exalted title manifesting some sort of basic moral quality. The major class differentiation on this measure was a tendency of middle-class persons to be a little more specific than working-class men.

As for opinions of 'religious belief', there were more significant variations by class, corresponding generally to the differences in rates of church participation. Slightly over half of the middle-class men expressed a decidedly high evaluation of religious belief while less than one-third of the working-class respondents did so. Most of the remainder of responses from all social groups were tolerant or non-committal toward religious belief; only 15% (quite evenly distributed by class) were unmistakably negative toward religious belief.

Since neither of the class divisions expressed deprecatory views of religious belief in as many as one-fifth of their answers, and since the vast majority of all groups were either tolerantly or positively supportive of the value of holding religious belief, we may conclude that, at an abstract level, there is general acceptance of religion. Mayor has made an incisive summary of the British religious conscience consistent with these findings:

> Open challenge to Christianity is not strong. . . . It is customary to say that the prevailing attitude is indifference to religion associated with naïve hedonism. . . . Religion of a sort is almost universal in Britain today; it is church-going and active participation which have failed.[18]

Zweig concluded from his interviews with English working-class men that, although most were religious believers in some way, '. . . . the nature of their belief was, in many cases, very vague and groping'.[19] Pickering also noted a certain superficial commendation of religious beliefs in England, using these phrases: 'Belief did not appear to motivate practice', and 'dogmatic assertions are of little importance'.[20]

Again, to speak impressionistically, the total volume of responses to such questions as these seemed to depict a tone of blandness surrounding matters of religion. Gone are the emotionally tinged doctrinal and ecclesiastical controversies that have marked the history of Scotland. Belief is not denounced or demeaned, but is viewed, on the whole, as a rather nebulous benefit and with a strong measure of tolerance. Perhaps the one term most clearly suggested by this tone is the word 'secular'. Religion is good, in the abstract, as to be a 'Christian' is good, in a vague way. But there is little excitement about either, positively or negatively. A vague, distant, respect for things religious prevails, but religious matters seem not to be of great consequence in the practical experience of most urban men.

To the statement, 'The Christian way is not the only way to know God', four out of five men gave their assent, further suggesting the general tolerance of religious attitudes. In fact, proportionately twice as many working-class men as middle-class men gave a dissenting opinion. This finding would seem to be somewhat at odds with the fact of much greater working-class abstention from the Church. But it is consistent with the profiles of responses to other doctrinal questions. For instance, on two questions most indicative of doctrinal 'orthodoxy', the working-class men were, in both cases, very slightly more orthodox than the middle-class men.

To look at these two measures specifically, almost four-fifths of the total sample agreed that 'Jesus is God's only Son' and just below two-fifths agreed with the proposition that 'The Bible is God's word and everything it says is completely true'. The general impression from these three doctrinal indices (and as already pointed out class differences were very minimal) is that while Christianity has by no means an exclusive claim on truth, the Divinity of Jesus is accepted as true, but the narrower 'inerrancy of the Bible' doctrine is considered optional and tenuous. Over two-thirds of all the men concurred with the proposition that 'living a good life is more important than having any particular religious belief'.

Clearly, religious belief, while vaguely salutary and beneficial, is not generally stressed as a prerequisite to 'the good life'. Similarly, in England, a Gallup survey found that 'only six per cent . . . directly attribute good behaviour to their religion'. Another indication which points toward the same conclusion is that two-thirds of the sample disagree completely with the suggestion that 'Christians ought to try to influence other people to think the way they do'. Again there was remarkable uniformity of response across class lines, with 5% more workers than non-manual persons taking the affirmative position. This again underlines the apparent pre-eminence of the norm of religious tolerance, which may be viewed as sub-species of secularization.

In his most fascinating and controversial volume, *The Secular City*, an American theologian, Harvey Cox, has developed the theme of secularization's impact on religious belief. He says:

> Secularization simply bypasses and undercuts religion and goes on to other things. It has relativized religious world-views and thus rendered them innocuous. . . . It has convinced the beliver that he *could* be wrong, and persuaded the devotee that there are more important things than dying for the faith. . . . Pluralism and tolerance are the children of secularization.[21]

Also from the American scene, where church attendance is much more widely practised than in Britain, a study of university students found that both the religious and the non-religious believe in a similar 'common cultural morality'.[22] Herberg argues that the three great American religious traditions, Catholic, Protestant and Jewish, are today mutually exalting a common cultural religion.[23] And Lenski suggests that, among Protestants in Detroit, 'a transcendental faith is gradually being transformed into a cultural faith'.[24]

A similar interpretation of religious trends in Scotland (and perhaps in Britain generally) is certainly plausible on the basis of this Edinburgh data. Indeed, strong supportive evidence – from the 'younger generation' – is adducible from a survey I conducted in six Edinburgh secondary schools. An 'open-ended' question asked simply that students indicate what they consider 'the two most important things in life'. Based upon a sample of 1110 secondary school students, only about 3% of the responses indicate values in any way related to religion. One is bound, I think, to interpret this remarkable paucity of religion-related responses as demonstrating that religious matters are, for the most part, low priorities among today's youth. Beyond the immediate significance, the apparent disregard of religion and Church among the younger generation seems to be a most negative augury for the Church in decades ahead. But, of course, such predictions are notoriously risky.

On a point related to the strength of religious values, Thompson, in his Birmingham inquiry, indicated that 'the appeal of the Church rests on social compatibility rather than doctrinal conviction'.[25] Whether secularization's advances are seen as encroachments upon the valued bastions of religious faith or as beneficial contributions to the climate of a complex, scientific age, there seems little doubt that these advances have eroded the dogmatic religious values of the past. Nor does this phenomenon appear to be specific to any class group. Paradoxically (considering rates of church involvement) working-class men reveal religious convictions a bit more to the orthodox end of the continuum than do middle-class men. Unmistakably, this evidence does not allow us to build an explanation for the wide class variations in overt religious practice in terms of class differences in religious belief systems.

Turning from elements of religiosity (in a generic sense) as indirect manifestations of the Church's current position in society, let us look now at some salient points of perception directly regarding the Church as an institution. In several ways, the respondents were asked to evaluate the Church 'in the large' – in terms of her total 'image'. In one approach, interviewees were asked to respond to the word 'church', using the technique of a modified psycho-analytical 'free association'. The results suggest that an appreciable vagueness shrouds the idea 'Church'. Revealingly, only one man thought first of a minister; in fact, few concrete images of any sort were elicited. Middle-class men were more specific than working-class men in denoting a location or particular activity associated with the Church;

but over-all, such replies accounted for less than one-fifth of the sample.

As was the case for 'religious belief', the Church was generally accorded a rather high evaluation in the abstract. With little variation between class groups, over three-fifths of the men mildly or strongly extolled the Church's putative worth. Most of the commendations were restrained and matter-of-fact, but none the less positive. One-fifth of the respondents, by contrast, issued forth invectives rather than accolades for the Church. However, looking more closely at the specific array of positive replies, one notices a striking absence of stress upon the communal aspects of church life–fellowship, emotional support of a close-knit of a close-knit group, mutual encouragement and friendship, etc. Whatever values are conceived as embodied in the Church, there is little perception of corporate solidarity. Only two men gave answers remotely connected with such values. I believe that this may throw a flash of light on the relative absence from the Church of lower-status social groups. Though the Church is considered abstractly worth while, she may provide mainly the opportunity for (to apply Toennies's well-known distinction) 'associational' involvement, without sufficient 'community' characteristics to translate (for most people) the vaguely positive evaluation into concrete church participation.

Responses to another query reinforced the above interpretation. Asked what they believe the Church 'ought to do for people', over half of the total number of respondents replied in a manner suggesting that the Church should expand her 'communal' values; she should relate herself more intimately and openly with people. Significantly, middle-class men placed rather less stress on this aspect than the manual workers. This is obviously in line with the theoretical model mentioned earlier, the church/sect distinction. If working-class persons have greater 'sect-like' religious propensities, desiring the succour of close-knit informal relationships rather than a formalized, liturgical church experience, and if the contemporary Church in Scotland is seen as overwhelmingly 'church-like' in character, this is, *prima facie*, a weighty factor in the large-scale working-class abstention. The whole institutional fabric of the Church, her total mode of operation, may thus be especially inimical to the character and focus of working-class 'life-style'. By contrast, there is a mountain of documentation for the notion that middle-class persons are great 'joiners'; they are oriented toward parti-

cipation in all sorts of 'formal associations' for specific satis-
factions.

Those who are concerned with making the Church increasingly
'relevant' to the modern, urban existence of all social classes, will
find little cause for encouragement from the following appraisals of
the Church's effectiveness and specific representations. The prevalent
feeling about the present 'fortunes' of the Church is that she is
decidedly waning; many seem ready to write the epitaph for institutional religion. Of the Prestonfield sample, 80% said the Church is
losing ground; only 7% described her as 'gaining ground'. In short,
while the Church is seen as upholding rather nebulous values she is
also viewed as unquestionably ineffective at the present time.

More specifically, the findings of this study point to a definite
attenuation of the esteem in which the Church's primary leaders,
ministers of religion, are held. Replies to questions about the typical
character and abilities possessed by the clergy create the impression
that ministers have been stripped of much of their once-hallowed
image. With little class-linked variation, only about one-third of
the men demonstrated a consistently high regard for ministers.
There was a volume of complaint against the 'dullness', insincerity,
and unawareness of the average minister, deriving from his pre-
sumed cloistered existence. Ministers are described as being 'closest
to' members of their own congregations, other church leaders, or
the more prosperous sections of the community. Rowntree and
Lavers, in their York survey, found that 'just a job' was a common
appraisal of the minister's role in society. They suggest that the clergy
often evoke hostility while the Church in general is regarded with
indifference.[26]

The common assertion that ministers have close personal relationships only with higher-status persons is unsurprising in light of the
predominantly middle-class composition of the churches and the
typically prosperous family backgrounds of the Scottish clergy.
Results of a postal questionnaire survey I distributed to Commissioners to the 1964 Church of Scotland General Assembly confirm
the built-in middle- and upper-class bias of the Scottish clergy.
Only 17% of the 260 ministers who responded described their fathers'
occupations as what can be classified as 'working-class'. Further,
only 20% indicated a political preference for the Labour Party,
perhaps a further indication of an 'élitist' view of the world.

Tom Allan, a famous Scottish minister, asserts this social 'distance'

between ministers and working class from the perspective of the
active clergyman enmeshed in the responsibilities of a busy parish:

> While I find it comparatively easy to mix with the professional and middle-
> class people of my parish and speak to them of the Faith, I find it inexpressibly
> hard to establish the same relationship among what are called the working-
> classes, although I was brought up in a working-class home. . . . We are
> strangers to our own people.[27]

While the profiles of responses regarding ministers do not con-
clusively differentiate between middle-class and working-class men,
the accurate awareness of the middle-class orientation of ministers
serves as another illuminating clue to the patterns of church involvement associated with the class groupings. Several comments from
workers in the sample epitomize the common opprobrium of such
perceptions:

> They are close to people with money. When a working man goes into church
> it's 'cheerio'; if I drove in with a Rolls Royce, they'd meet me and show me
> to the front seat.

> Usually it's the middle class they're next to. I don't think they have much
> time for ordinary working-class people.

> They're out for rich people, to try to get on the right side of these people.

Closely related was a question pertaining to the class position of
church-goers generally. With virtually identical response patterns
for working-class and middle-class groups, three-fifths of the over-
all sample describe the typical church composition as primarily
middle-class. Only 17% see the composition as working-class
primarily; the remainder are unsure or detect no class discrepancies
in church participation. Many of those describing church-goers as
middle-class added comments maligning the motives involved in
church attendance. Such epithets as 'It's a show', 'put on', 'phoney',
'a place to conduct business', 'all to give an impression', were
frequently expressed.

A similar extensive array of deprecatory remarks appeared when
interviewees were asked to describe 'the people who go to church
regularly'. While one-third of the men extolled church-goers as
'Christians' or exceptionally good persons, the remainder were
persuaded that church-going proceeds on the basis of mere habit or
motives even less deserving of approbation, such as rank hypocrisy.
Paradoxically, middle-class men were even more critical than
working-class men, despite the higher rates of middle-class church
attendance. Not even the church-goers themselves were free of

suspicion regarding the character traits of church-goers; in fact, those who had described themselves as frequent attenders viewed church-goers with more disapproval than those who are non-participants in the church. On another measure, fewer than 30% of the total sample expressed the view that the lives of church-goers compare favourably with those who abstain from church. Most were convinced that there is simply no noticeable difference associated with the practice of church involvement at all. Likewise, a Gallup survey in England found that only 13% of the members of the Church of England thought that church-goers lead better lives.[28]

A final manifestation of the Church which elicited a revealing commentary on prevailing attitudes may be referred to as the Church's 'programme' – church services and other activities sponsored by the Church. Respondents were asked to describe their impressions of Sunday services, for instance. Two-fifths, over all, were in some regard favourable to the atmosphere or effects of church worship services; the remaining three-fifths expressed negative opinions ranging from mild assertions of the 'dullness' of services to strong verbal rebukes concerning the antiquated style or irrelevance of the services. Commonly, the sermons were singled out for criticism.

The general profile of answers suggested that whether an individual felt 'comfortable' inside the church architecture or not, there is a serious breakdown in communication, as if a great chasm separates pulpit from pew; as if the phrases of religious piety voiced on Sunday morning seem to bear meagre relationship to the problems of everyday existence. Of course, such a suggestion is so common today as to be trite, but this one survey did seem to support its reality in the perception of Edinburgh men.

Compatible with the above interpretation is the further fact that three-fifths of the interviewees believe that 'the church is too formal'. Also, 70% over-all, with especially strong working-class concurrence, supported the idea that the Church should initiate informal forums of discussion and fellowship, in which persons could interact and freely relate the teachings of the Church to pressing matters of life. I was struck by the fact that the regular church-goers of the sample were largely without close interpersonal ties with their fellow church participants. So, again, the image of the Church as thoroughly 'associational' and non-communal is brought into focus. Yinger makes the incisive point that the Church, unlike many other organizations, in order to accomplish her goals effectively, '. . . ordinarily requires the active co-operation of the whole range of membership'.[29] It has been proposed that the relative 'success' of the American churches derives from the systems of interaction and attachments to meaningful groups that have been developed within church organizations.[30]

Asked for suggested changes in the Church which would make her more 'attractive' to people, the Edinburgh men once more emphasized 'communal' goals. They also stressed the need for a 'brighter, livelier' approach to religion. While such responses accounted for over half the total answers, the working-class men expressed such views nearly twice as often as middle-class men. Thus, from a slightly different angle, the overwhelming estrangement of working-class men from the forms and atmosphere of institutional religion again stands in relief.

In summary, we have noted a remarkable unanimity of attitudes toward the Church among working-class and middle-class men. There is a much higher degree of approval of the Church (and religion) in the abstract than there is of certain conspicuous manifestations of the Church such as ministers, church-goers and church services. On the face of it this is a paradox. With regard to its general 'value', and in terms of minimal doctrinal commitments, religion is the recipient of respectful deference. Few are anti-Church or anti-religion on an ideological plane. Tolerance is regnant.

Perhaps, in the abstract the Church and her belief system represent the general value system (and moral norms) of society at large – a sort of social norm writ in religious symbols. To this extent, and in a rather distant way, she is a revered institution, an accepted and valued feature of the social landscape. But when more concrete expressions of the Church are brought into consideration, only a minority are willing to eulogize the Church in a similar way. This curious contradiction between abstract appraisal of the Church and attitudes directly pertinent to the institutional operation of the Church seems to me a significantly revealing commentary on the position of the Church in contemporary society.

Despite the uniformity of church 'attachment' profiles across class lines, certain key clues have emerged which, at least speculatively, serve as the basis of explanation for the relative working-class abstention from the Church. First, we have already noted the relevance of the 'church/sect' theoretical model. The widely perceived lack of 'communal' characteristics in the Church of Scotland, and the formalized and 'associational' pattern that obtains with her, may make her particularly uncongenial to working-class persons. Working-class life style, with its basis in informal structures of interpersonal relations and its 'immediacy' of content, is perhaps largely incompatible with the major institutional forms of religion. Secondly, the accurate conception of the Church as middle-class in orientation, composition and leadership may serve as another basis of working-class estrangement from the Church.

Of course, it will be readily detected that this set of tentative explanations begs certain other questions, especially historical questions. If middle-class dominance in the Church of Scotland is a current fact, what is the genesis of this situation? And if the putative 'sect-type' propensities of the working classes are not compatible with the 'church-type' character of the dominant religious organizations, why have the working-classes not, on the whole, become actively engaged in sectarian religious milieux? Unfortunately, the scope of this paper does not allow for thorough investigation of these further matters. But let it be suggested briefly that the present church-class configuration is rooted in the sweeping social changes of the early nineteenth century. In a sense, the urban working classes have not been 'lost' to the Church, as is commonly supposed. The Church never did command the commitment of the plethora of rural folk who swarmed into the dismal inner-city areas of the burgeoning nineteenth-century cities.

During this dynamic era of industrial transformation, the Church was thoroughly enamoured with the 'bourgeois' world view and she became virtually a spokesman for the ascendant classes. To those who were impoverished and degraded by the oppressive conditions of the period – which are as dramatically portrayed by Dickens as by Marx – the Church had little more to offer than moralistic pronouncements. Poverty was seen, in a unique amalgam of John Calvin and Adam Smith, as the outcome of personal moral degeneracy. Few had any awareness that the blighted conditions of individuals and groups could be generated by massive structural changes in society; that personal troubles could be rooted in large-scale 'social problems'. Needless to say, the platitudes of personal piety rang exceedingly hollow and hypocritical to many of those caught in the vicious cycle of squalor, disease and abject poverty.

On a more practical level, also, the Church was unprepared in that critical period (in terms of her allocation of resources, organization and perspectives) to respond expeditiously to the demands of population shifts which were unprecedented and explosive. She could not maintain contact with persons in the myriad new milieux of the crowded industrial cities for several crucial decades. The new urban working classes were therefore ignored, slighted and estranged by the Church – perhaps irretrievably. In short, urban working-class culture has never viably included the practice of regular church-attendance as a prevalent custom. When the 'proletariat' did seek redress for its invidiously oppressed situation, the efforts were mainly at the secular level of the Labour Movement rather than in the religious solutions of sectarian fervour.

While the foregoing historical sketch does no more than hint at the relevant rootage of the current class-church relationship, it is perhaps enough to demonstrate that the historical-structural level of sociological analysis is a necessary counterpart of the 'social-psychological' approach for interpretative understanding of the question posed in this paper as well as for most important sociological questions. It is essential to deal with social forces at several levels – not only at the levels of individual perceptions and the character of small-scale milieux, but also at the level of historical alterations in the structural configurations of society, including changes in the major institutional forms and the relationships between them. The ramifications and consequences of these larger social forces generally escape the awareness of individuals whose lives are so greatly shaped by them.

Insights emerging from the Edinburgh survey are, I think, illuminating with regard to the current 'image' and position of the Church in society and with regard to certain interpretations of the wide class disparities in church participation. However, working-class estrangement from the Church and the diminishing importance of the Church generally, along with concomitant phenomena such as secularization, must also be seen in a larger historical frame of reference in order to approach comprehensive understanding. The present brief paper must, therefore, be confined to partial interpretations and a few insights which one hopes will be useful.

NOTES

1. There was an additional residual category composed of respondents whose occupations were not clearly manual or non-manual. This small intermediate group (of only seventeen men) will not be singled out in the discussions that follow.

2. Ernst Troeltsch, *The Social Teaching of the Christian Churches*, English translation by Olive Wyon, London: Allen and Unwin, and New York: Macmillan, 1931; reprinted New York: Harper Torchbooks, 1960.

3. N. J. Demerath III, *Social Class in American Protestantism*, Chicago: Rand McNally, 1965.

4. Charles Glock and Rodney Stark, *Religion and Society in Tension*, New York: Rand McNally, 1965.

5. *Op. cit.*, p. 19.

6. John Highet, *The Scottish Churches: A Review of their State 400 Years After the Reformation*, London: Skeffington, 1960, p. 61.

7. See, for instance, *Mass Observation*, 'Meet Yourself on Sunday', Naldrett Press, 1949, p. 3; Social Surveys (Gallup Poll) Ltd., *Television and Religion*, University of London Press, 1964; Michael Argyle, *Religious Behaviour*, London: Routledge and Kegan Paul, 1958; T. Cauter and J. S. Downham, *The Communication of Ideas*, London: Chatto and Windus, 1954.

8. Benson Y. Landis, *Religion in the United States*, New York: Barnes and Noble, Inc., 1955, p. 108; Bernard Lazerwitz, 'Religion and Social Structure in the United States', in Louis Schneider (ed.), *Religion, Culture and Society: A Reader in the Sociology of Religion*, New York: John Wiley and Sons, 1964.

9. E. R. Wickham, *Church and People in an Industrial City*, London: Lutterworth Press, 1957, p. 217.

10. R. H. T. Thompson, *The Church's Understanding of Itself: A Study of Four Birmingham Parishes*, London: SCM Press, 1957, p. 83.

11. For instance, Michael Argyle, *op. cit.*, p. 130; Peter Willmott, *The Evolution of a Community: A Study of Dagenham after Forty Years*, London: Routledge and Kegan Paul, 1963, p. 140.

12. Abbé G. Michonneau, *Revolution in a City Parish*, London: Blackfriars, 1949, p. xx.

13. Emile Pin, S.J., *Pratique Religieuse et Classes Sociales Dans Une Paroisse Urbaine Saint-Pothin à Lyon*, Paris: Editions Spes, 1956; quoted from translation in Schneider (ed.), *op. cit.*, p. 416.

14. François-André Isambert, *Christianisme et Classes Ouvrières* (Casterman, 1961), translated and condensed in Schneider, *op. cit.*, p. 400.

15. Gerhard Lenski, *The Religious Factor: A Sociological Study of Religion's Impact on Politics, Economics and Family Life*, Garden City, New York: Anchor Books, 1963, p. 48; and Bernard Lazerwitz, 'Some Factors Associated with Variations in Church Attendance', *Social Forces*, May 1961, pp. 301–09; Lee G. Burchinal, 'Some Social Status Criteria and Church Membership and Church Attendance', *Journal of Social Psychology*, 1959, pp. 53–64.

16. Gibson Winter, *The Suburban Captivity of the Churches: An Analysis of Protestant Responsibility in the Expanding Metropolis*, New York: Doubleday, and London: SCM Press, 1961, p. 45.

17. Thompson, *op. cit.*, p. 12.

18. S. H. Mayor, 'The Religion of the British People', *Hibbert Journal 59*, 1960, pp. 38–43.

19. Ferdinand Zweig, *The Worker in an Affluent Society*, London: Heinemann, 1961, p. 146.

20. W. S. F. Pickering, 'Religious Movements of Church Members in Two Working Class Towns in England', *Archives de Sociologie des Religions* 11, Jan.-June 1961, pp. 129–40.

21. Harvey Cox, *The Secular City: Secularization and Urbanization in Theological Perspective*, New York: Macmillan, and London: SCM Press, 1965, pp. 2–3.

22. Russell Middleton and Putney Snell, 'Religion, Normative Standards, and Behavior', *Sociometry 25*, June 1962, pp. 141–52.

23. Will Herberg, *Protestant, Catholic, Jew: An Essay in American Religious Sociology*, New York: Doubleday Anchor Books, 1960.

24. Gerhard Lenski, *op. cit.*, p. 59.

25. Thompson, *op. cit.*, p. 85.

26. B. S. Rowntree and G. R. Lavers, *English Life and Leisure: A Social Study*, London: Longman, 1951, pp. 346, 349, 352.

27. Thomas Allan, *The Face of My Parish*, London: SCM Press, 1954, p. 107.

28. Social Surveys (Gallup Poll), *op. cit.*, p. 54.

29. Milton Yinger, *Sociology Looks at Religion*, New York: Macmillan, 1963, p. 178.

30. John D. Photadis, 'Overt Conformity to Church Teaching as a Function of Religious Belief and Group Participation', *American Journal of Sociology*, 1965.

2 Bureaucracy and the Church

Kenneth Thompson

THE dysfunctions of bureaucracy in religious organizations have been a constant theme for discussion in contemporary religious circles, especially in the Church of England since the publication in 1964 of Leslie Paul's report on the deployment and payment of the clergy.[1] It is all the more surprising, therefore, that so little attention has been paid to this problem by professional sociologists.[2] This paper will be devoted to making some suggestions as to how sociological theory and research might assist in bringing greater clarity and objectivity into that debate. The suggestions are formulated on the basis of experience gained in doing research into the development of those forms of organization in the Church of England which have most frequently been termed bureaucratic.[3]

Whilst accepting the importance and relevance of many of the criticisms of bureaucracy in religious organizations, I would like to play the devil's advocate for a while and, to start with, try to suggest some of the valuable functions that formal organization, of the type that Max Weber taught us to call bureaucratic, might be serving.[4] After all, it cannot be unreasonable for a sociologist to be interested in the reasons for the extension and persistence of traits which, in some of their aspects, appear so antithetical to the pure values and goals of most religious ideologies. Their manifest functions in terms of potential efficiency and ability to satisfy the material requirements of a religious organization, especially in a period of rapid social change when planned adaptation is necessary, are not difficult to discern. These manifest functions are obviously made possible by bureaucracy's utilization of formally rational criteria, involving the translation of issues into numerical, calculable terms. Some of the less appreciated functions of bureaucracy can also be related to its institutionalized commitment to the utilization of formally rational criteria in its operations. Such criteria have the advantage of being relatively uncontroversial, or at least more explicit, when compared with those involved in making decisions about the substantial rationality of different courses of action.

The distinction between formal and substantive rationality as set out in Weber's discussion of sociological categories of economic action, suggest why this should be so.

A system of economic activity will be called 'formally' rational according to the degree in which the provision for needs, which is essential to every rational economy, is capable of being expressed in numerical, calculable terms, and is so expressed. . . .

On the other hand, the concept of substantive rationality is full of difficulties. It conveys only one element common to all the possible empirical situations; namely, that it is not sufficient to consider only the purely formal fact that calculations are being made on grounds of expediency by the methods which are, among those available, technically the most nearly adequate. In addition it is necessary to take account of the fact that economic activity is oriented to ultimate ends (*Forderungen*) of some kind, whether they be ethical, political, utilitarian, hedonistic, the attainment of social distinction, of social equality, or of anything else. Substantive rationality cannot be measured in terms of formal calculation alone, but also involves a relation to the absolute values or to the content of the particular given ends to which it is oriented. In principle, there is an indefinite number of possible standards of value which are 'rational' in this sense.[5]

Because a religious body is primarily an ideological institution, concerned with the promulgation and application of certain values and ideals, there is a great deal of scope for internal disagreement and dissatisfaction over the methods to be employed for translating theory into practice, ideals into policy. What Weber described as possible in principle – an indefinite number of possible standards of value which are substantively rational – in large, heterogeneous churches or denominations, of which the Church of England is a good example, is also likely to be experienced as a paralysing reality when different theological parties or other groups offer rival policies. At such times a bureaucratic form of organization, and 'expert' advice, may be turned to with relief by the leaders, because it is generally believed to be relatively neutral and impartial, by reason of its commitment to the principles of formal rationality. Thus on occasions when policy decisions have been urgently required in the Church of England, it has sometimes happened that the responsibility for making the decision has had to be borne by officials of the Central Board of Finance or the Church Commissioners. This has brought them much criticism, even though more discerning critics have acknowledged that the responsibility had to be borne by the

B

officials because the Church could not reach agreement to make the decisions in any other way.[6]

However, it is far from the case that bureaucrats have too large an appetite for such decision-making; the reverse is more likely to be true – that they dislike having to make policy decisions, because this exposes them to criticism and excessive public scrutiny. The Committee on Central Funds, which investigated the departments of the Church Assembly in the 1950s, found that the Central Board of Finance had often been faced with the choice of making decisions which were in fact decisions on policy, or else letting the Assembly and the departments go their own way. The Central Board protested that it was not a suitable or competent body to determine policy, and it admitted that it had often taken the line of least resistance.[7]

The commitment of bureaucracy to norms of efficiency and expertise, and its structural characteristics of clearly defined hierarchy of offices and spheres of competence, separation of the official from the ownership of the means of administration, and recruitment on the basis of technical qualifications, with fixed salaries, full-time employment, and a career structure based on seniority or achievement, can also serve to give the organization at least an outward appearance of modernity. In this respect bureaucracy serves the function of commending the Church to the general public as an institution which is not afraid to move with the times – a not unimportant consideration in a period of rapid social change. This type of organizational change in the nineteenth century reduced the Church of England's vulnerability to charges of nepotism (if not of social bias). It also enabled it to interact more easily, and to transact business, with those similar structures which had appeared in other fields of organization – government, business, education, and the like. To some extent it was able to attract well-qualified laymen into its full-time service by offering them regular (if not well-paid) careers, although the different origins of the Church Commissioners and the Church Assembly departments, the two main central administrative agencies in the Church of England, have produced significantly different results in this respect.[8]

Despite the manifest and subsidiary functions of bureaucratic forms of organization, it is the dysfunctional aspect of bureaucracy that is most firmly established in the public mind, and especially in the minds of churchmen. Although sociologists claim to use the term 'bureaucracy' in a neutral, technical sense, they cannot escape from bearing some of the responsibility for the increasing ambiguity which pervades the concept (referring indiscriminately, as it now does, to both forms and faults of organization).

It was indicative of the confusion when the French sociologist Michel Crozier had to begin his recent book, *The Bureaucratic Phenomenon*, by pointing out how vague the term 'bureaucratic' had become.[9] At least three major uses could be distinguished. Firstly, there was its most traditional usage as it derived from the political sphere, in which it referred to government by bureaux – departments staffed by appointed and not elected functionaries, organized hierarchically and dependant on a sovereign authority. Secondly, there was Max Weber's usage, as propagated by sociologists and historians, in which bureaucratization referred to the rationalization of collective activities. Finally, there was bureaucracy in its vulgar sense of slowness, ponderousness, routine, complication of procedures, and maladapted response of the organization to the needs it is supposed to satisfy. The confusion has been increased by the fact that sociologists have not confined themselves to the second usage, and neither have critics of bureaucracy in the Church and other institutions remained content with the items listed under the vulgar usage.

Probably the only time that 'bureaucracy' enjoyed the status of a univocal concept was in the eighteenth century, when the French minister of commerce, Vincent de Gournay, first envisaged the public offices as the operating government by speaking of it as *bureaucratie*.[10] Thus it was that in the first half of the nineteenth century the term still did not feature in criticisms of organizational developments in the Church of England. When the conservative Bishop Phillpotts wished to make such criticisms of the Ecclesiastical Commissioners, for instance, he adopted the same policy as *The Times*, and included them all in the blanket term 'centralization', which they condemned as both foreign to the English language and to the habits of the English nation.[11] In the second half of the nineteenth century the term 'bureaucracy' began to take on its second meaning of referring to a specific form or structure of organization, especially in references by German scholars to *Bürokratie*. Max Weber later presented an elaborate characterization of these aspects of bureaucracy in terms of hierarchy, jurisdiction, specialization, professional training, fixed compensation, and permanence. Unfortunately, despite the fruitfulness of this usage for Weber's own purpose of utilizing historical materials in social science, and for inspiring a succession of sociological studies of bureaucracy, this 'ideal type' bureaucracy has also rendered the term even more ambiguous.[12]

The reason for this is that the type is not built up by deduction from higher concepts which have been previously established, nor is it abstracted from empirical data through the method of concomitant variations in a way that would produce working hypotheses from the data. By constructing his ideal type on the basis of a one-sided exaggeration of a great many diffuse and discrete phenomena Weber gave rise to the habit of regarding these phenomena as linked together in one unitary type. In other words, far from assisting in discriminating between different classes of phenomena, such as the structural, behavioural and purposive aspects of an organization, the ideal type tempts us to assume that they automatically appear together.

Although Weber made strenuous efforts to develop a *wertfreie Wissenschaft* – a social science free of value judgements – he could not prevent his own liberal instincts from affecting his discussion of bureaucracy. He identified bureaucracy with rationality, and the process of rationalization with mechanism, depersonalization, and oppressive routine, and, as such, adverse to personal freedom. He saw it all as part of the unilinear development of rationalization and demystification (*Entzauberung der Welt*) in the modern world. Weber's influence has been widespread among sociologists, who have in turn influenced the wider public in its theorizing about bureaucracy, if only because sociologists' interest in the pathology of organizations has given the impression that organizational growth, the increase of administrative staff, and such dysfunctions as formalism, impersonality, and the displacement of goals, are all part of a single trend. This has given rise to a 'metaphysical pathos' with regard to bureaucracy – a mood of pessimism and fatalism.[13]

If even sociologists occasionally fall victims to metaphysical pathos with regard to bureaucracy, it should not surprise us if churchmen exhibit a similar tendency. It should be a matter of concern, however, when sociological concepts are transformed into ideological weapons, and this is what has happened in some debates on organizational change in the Church of England. Of course the Church is not the only institution in which this occurs, but it is particularly susceptible to it because it is primarily an ideological institution, concerned with the promulgation of particular ideas, and consequently its personnel (especially professionals) have ideological commitments which are more articulate and more determining in their influence on the members' perception of the organization. It is difficult for the religious practitioner to analyse even administrative agencies, where formal rationality is maximized, without placing them in the familiar context of the dialectic between doctrine and polity, faith and practice.

It is easy to accept in principle that polity is the sociological manifestation of doctrine, or the political expression of the content of the gospel, but the consequences are often less palatable. That part of the polity which is responsible for administrative functions has to operate within the limitations imposed by various external constraints (such as relations with other institutions, including the state), scarcity of resources for competing ends, and the need to take note of all the different claims made on it by groups and individuals asserting the primacy of divergent goals, values, and status concerns. Failure to satisfy any of these claims may produce criticism which does not confine itself to the specific issue, but which extends itself into a blanket condemnation of bureaucracy, on the grounds that the form and rationality of bureaucratic organization can never truly express the Church's theology.

None of these remarks are intended to suggest that bureaucratic forms of organization do not have dysfunctional consequences for religious bodies. On the contrary, it is being suggested that a realistic appraisal of bureaucracy and its effects (including dysfunction) can only be achieved if the various components are carefully distinguished. Unless this is carried out 'bureaucracy' as a concept will continue to hinder rather than assist an accurate estimation of the real roots of the problems encountered in religious organizations. In the past, on the frequent occasions when the term 'bureaucracy' has featured in discussions of such problems in the Church of England, it has been used simply as a blanket condemnation of a whole trend or area of organization. Far from solving the problems inherent in church administration, this kind of condemnation instead leads to greater secretiveness, defensiveness, and uncertainty among the administrators. The prediction of increasing bureaucratization, in its dysfunctional aspects, then begins to function as a self-fulfilling prophecy, giving rise to those behavioural patterns that it criticizes. Lacking an organization theory that would help them to understand themselves, and in the absence of a theology of organization that would legitimize their necessary power in the eyes of the Church, the more vulnerable departments of the organization fail to demonstrate the one virtue that Max Weber attributed to bureaucracy – superior efficiency.

All the main departments in the central administration of the Church of England have gone through this experience to some extent during their history. The most severe accusations of bureaucratic behaviour seem to be levelled at them during their early, formative years, and it has frequently produced the self-fulfilling prophecy effect discussed above. The Ecclesiastical Commissioners had to answer such charges before select committees once every decade for the first thirty years of their existence.[14] It was in this period of constant criticism that it most manifested the character of a bureaucracy in its vulgar sense of slowness, ponderousness, routine, complication of procedures, and maladapted response to many of the needs it was supposed to satisfy (especially that of raising clergy stipends – as the lower clergy bitterly pointed out). Since that time, and most notably since it merged with the older Queen Anne's Bounty in 1947 to become the Church Commissioners for England, it has become increasingly efficient (especially in raising clergy stipends) and so less criticized. However, its earlier experience of criticism and its defensive reaction has left its mark – so much so that one recent critic has described it as 'almost neurotically sensitive about criticism', and accuses it of working according to the strictest interpretation of its brief, which means taking no initiatives and launching no experiments.[15]

The Ecclesiastical Commissioners were most criticized during the period when they lacked the necessary funds and technical knowledge to be able to translate the various claims made on them into the numerical, calculable terms which are essential to every rational economy. Once they were able to utilize the principles of formal rationality to a sufficient degree, by virtue of their gradual accumulation of funds and technical knowledge, then their manifest efficiency began to earn for them a kind of 'expediential authority' – an authority which derives its legitimacy not from a theology of organization, nor from ecclesiastical tradition, but primarily from the ability to achieve assigned goals arising out of the immediate needs of the Church.[16]

The Church Assembly departments have a similar history, although in most of their cases they have been so limited in funds and qualified personnel that they have not, so far, been able to attain the same degree of efficiency, success, and so authority, as the Church Commissioners. (Also, they do not play any part in supplementing clergy stipends), which might at least have brought them some popularity.) Within five years of the inception of the Church Assembly the Bishop of Exeter was writing in *The Church Assembly News* that the Church was 'creating a bureaucratic government' and that 'bureaucracy is the certain result of an exaggerated centralization of government'. The bureaucratic features that he listed included: harshness of government or 'red-tapism', which he described as 'an effort to govern different people in different conditions by one rule'; incapacity for experimentation ('history has always credited bureaucratic government with an almost paralytic impotence to accommodate itself to changes that a changing world demands'); extravagance; rigidity; and lack of enterprise.[17] To those who worked in the Church Assembly offices at the time (1924), with their small staff and declining budget, such fears must have seemed totally unwarranted – as the secretary of the Central Board of Finance pointed out in a subsequent rejoinder.[18] Nevertheless the same fears have been repeatedly expressed, and although the Church Assembly organization has been denied some of the resources necessary to develop all the structural components of bureaucracy (in its more neutral and sociological sense), uncertainty and defensiveness have once again produced some dysfunctional, behavioural consequences.[19] The report of an investigation carried out by the Organization and Methods Division of the Treasury in 1954–55, whilst criticizing these defensive practices, implied that far from being a powerful bureaucracy, the organization was understaffed and, in some cases overworked and underpaid.

The reasons for the constant use (or misuse) of the term 'bureaucracy' and its earlier synonym 'centralization' should be of interest not only to the academic sociologist, but also to all those churchmen who seek to understand the real nature of recent organizational developments and the problems which they pose for the Church. The first step in reaching such an understanding must be to separate out the different meanings which 'bureaucracy' has for those who use it as a criticism.

At least four broad meanings can be distinguished: (1) bureaucracy as a particular form of organization with its own distinctive rationality; (2) bureaucracy as an ailment of organization, or as faults in organization, which obstructs effective operation; (3) bureaucracy in the sense of 'big government' or centralization; and (4) bureaucracy as a blight, always for the worst, falling on liberty and individuality. Different groups and individuals who are critical of the organizational changes taking place in the Church, invest the term 'bureaucracy' with those meanings which most emphasize their immediate concerns. A group or an individual concerned primarily with the need to stress the distinctive values of the religious institution is likely to object to the form or rationality of bureaucracy because it threatens to undermine those values.[21] Those responsible for providing instrumental leadership in the Church will confine their concern about 'bureaucracy' to those defects of organization which obstruct effective operation. Groups with local interests view bureaucracy as 'big government' or centralization, which overrides those interests. Individuals who prize their freedom or professional independence feel anxious about the effect of bureaucracy on their liberty or status.

Often it happens that critics intend to include all or several of these meanings in their references to bureaucracy, but more often they have some specific concern which can be related to their own standpoint or position in the Church. The real nature of their objections to particular developments in church organization can best be understood if these factors are taken into account. Thus the objections to the Ecclesiastical Commissioners' 'centralization' of church administration in the nineteenth century were not the same thing when made by theologians of the Oxford Movement as they were when advanced by deans and chapters. The Oxford Movement objected to the new organization because of the primacy which it seemed to give to formally rational criteria to the neglect of considerations of divine ordinance and the distinctive values and character of the Church as an institution. Deans and chapters objected to centralization because it tended to override local interests and customs. Some of the clergy's objections to the Paul Report's proposals can be seen to have stemmed not only from dislike of bureaucracy as a form of organization with its own distinctive rationality, but also from a fear of the consequences of such organization for the clergy's status. It was along these lines that a clergyman in the Anglican journal *Parish and People* complained that the reader of the Paul Report 'is left with the unmistakable impression that the organization referred to is a bureaucracy and not a fellowship of Christian Believers'. He then ended his article by adding that: 'Finally, the tackling of the problem of stipends by each diocese individually, resulting in the enhancement of the status of the parochial clergy (without any pillaging of trust funds) would do more for the C. of E. than any of Mr Paul's 62 proposals.'[22]

Until the various structural components of bureaucracy are more clearly distinguished and the causal relationships with behavioural aspects are established, it will be impossible to substitute accurate evaluation of the effects of organizational developments for the prevailing pessimism and fatalism in the Church. Just how great a hindrance this presents to constructive reform was exemplified by the reception given to the report of the committee which investigated the working of the Church Assembly organization and presented its findings in 1956. This Committee on Central Funds found that the Assembly had a large number of more or less autonomous boards and councils, many of which were descended from bodies previously entirely independent, and which had been adopted or created by the Assembly without any attempt at comprehensive planning. In the Committee's view the organization was not only unsatisfactory in its scope, but it was also too inflexible to be capable of the rapid and easy self-adjustment which a constantly changing situation required. It stated that greater flexibility could be achieved by the use of general directives rather than by rigid constitutions, and by the exercise of a greater measure of co-ordination than was possible in the existing arrangement. The Committee therefore recommended that most of the existing twenty-two departments should be merged or grouped under four major departments, and that these should then be directly represented on a strengthened and enlarged standing committee of the Assembly. In this way the Committee hoped to carry out a much-needed rationalization of the organization and also secure more adequate co-ordination and control of its activities.

The Committee's report anticipated that rationalization would be equated with bureaucratization and so it explicitly stated that: 'What is required at the centre, therefore, is not an authoritarian bureaucracy but an organization existing for the mutual advantage of the dioceses, adequately controlled, and sufficiently flexible to be capable of easy and rapid adjustment. . . .'[23] Despite this statement making clear that the proposals were aimed at eliminating precisely those characteristic of bureaucracy which are agreed to be dysfunctional, the ensuing debate in the Church Assembly was thrown into confusion by denunciations of bureaucracy. The prevailing tone was set by a speech from one of the bishops, who said that the Church of

England was in danger of being organized too much as a business firm. His statement that there had been too much of the 'Americanization' process suggested that there had been little progress in the discussion since Bishop Phillpotts denounced such 'foreign' notions.[24]

Sociologists and churchmen each have a contribution to make if any advance is to be made. Sociologists can begin by making some kind of distinction, along the lines already suggested by S. N. Eisenstadt, between the growth of bureaucracy and the growth of bureaucratization. According to Eisenstadt the former should refer to the development of bureaucratic organizations in society, and the latter to the extension of the power of a bureaucratic organization over many areas beyond its initial purpose, and its regimentation of these areas. He suggested that the conditions conducive to the growth of bureaucracy and the growth of bureaucratization are very different. The first are societal in nature (extensive differentiation of institutional spheres, universalistic achievement criteria for role occupancy, etc.).[25] In this respect the growth of bureaucratic organization in the Church of England can be analysed as part of the process of institutional differentiation in English society. At the beginning of the nineteenth century the Church of England had a traditional structure that was closely intertwined at all levels with the other institutions of society. Since the Reform Era and the creation of the Ecclesiastical Commissioners, however, the Church has received delegated powers from the state for its own officers and agencies, so that administrative action inside the Church has increased. To that extent there has been an increase in formal, bureaucratic organization, especially in those areas involving fund raising and budgeting in which servicing and support from central and local government was reduced or withdrawn. Bureaucracy in this sense can be regarded simply as a tool created for the efficient implementation of set goals. As such it needs encouragement to become the epitome of rationality for the purpose of attaining its goals and providing required services. The term 'bureaucratization' would then be reserved for describing a process by which a bureaucracy extends its activities and power beyond those limits necessary for implementing its set goals, and where it displaced its service goals in favour of various power interests. And as the Committee on Central Funds perceived, this is less likely to occur where control is vested in a strong, representative executive.

Sociological analysis needs to go even further than the simple operation of distinguishing between bureaucracy and bureaucratization, however, if it is to be of much assistance in furthering the Church's understanding of its organization. It must also go on to break down the composite type 'bureaucracy' into its various components so that the relationships between those elements become a matter for empirical investigation and not a matter of *a priori* postulation. It might then be possible to translate the insights and assertions of Max Weber regarding bureaucracy and its effects into testable hypotheses about the relationships between structural variables like specialization of function, standardization of procedures and roles, formalization of written procedures, centralization of decision-making, configuration of authority structure, and flexibility of structure, and on the other hand the several behavioural variables.[26]

Churchmen on their part could reciprocate by showing their willingness to use these sharpened conceptual tools for the proper purpose of objective analysis, instead of blunting them by misusing them as ideological weapons. They should also be prepared to recognize some of the motivation behind such misuse. In some cases it would be seen to be a symptom of reluctance to face up to internal contradictions within the doctrinal system, which is often the real cause of the dilemmas experienced by a church when it attempts to express its beliefs through its polity. The failure to develop an accepted theology of organization bears witness to this. As one Church Assembly administrator has put it: 'What is our *theology* of administration – of the committee, the report, the meeting, the letter? If we don't have a theology, we shall be drawn by the world into bureaucracy.'[27]

Of course, if the Church did resolve its dilemmas there is always the possibility that the resulting polity might be of a type that excluded large-scale organization altogether – as would be the case in a congregation-centred, sect type of organization. Bureaucracy might then be no longer a problem. Until such a time, however, the most positive course of action must be to seek to evaluate the real facts about bureaucracy and its dysfunctions for a religious body, rather than using it as a scapegoat for other failures in the Church.

It may be that the role of scapegoat is the chief, and most burdensome, latent function that bureaucracy serves in religious bodies. It has been said of the Church Assembly by a member of its Standing Committee that 'It is often blamed for not doing what it was never intended to do, and I think that there are times when it fulfils the role of scapegoat for failures which have their origins in other quarters'.[28] But although the use of a scapegoat can bring some psychological relief, it cannot remove the causes of failure (a lesson which theologians are accustomed to teach). It would seem that the only alternative to facing the *facts* about bureaucracy is to succumb to metaphysical pathos.

NOTES

1. Leslie Paul, *The Development and Payment of the Clergy*, London: Church Information Office, 1964.

2. Notable exceptions include Bryan R. Wilson, 'The Paul Report Examined', in *Theology*, No. 536, Feb. 1965, pp. 89–103; Paul M. Harrison, *Authority and Power in the Free Church Tradition*, Princeton University Press, 1959; and Charles H. Page, 'Bureaucracy and the Liberal Church', in *The Review of Religion* 16, Nov. 1951, pp. 137–50.

3. The results of that research are to be found in K. A. Thompson, *The Organizational Response of the Church of England to Social Change, with Particular Reference to Developments Associated with the Church Assembly*, unpublished D.Phil. Thesis, Oxford University, 1967.

4. According to Weber, bureaucracy involves a clear-cut division of integrated activities which are regarded as duties inherent in the office. Assignment of roles is on the basis of technical qualifications which are ascertained through formalized impersonal procedures (e.g. examinations). Within the structure of hierarchically arranged authority, the activities of trained and salaried experts are governed by general, abstract, clearly defined rules, which preclude the necessity for the issuance of specific instructions for each case. This generality of the rules necessitates categorization, so that individual problems and cases are classified on the basis of designated criteria and treated accordingly. (Max Weber, *The Theory of Social and Economic Organization*, trans. A. M. Henderson and Talcott Parsons, New York: The Free Press, paperback edn. 1964, pp. 329–37.) In the case of the central administrative agencies of the Church of England, the extent to which each of them possessed these attributes varies.

5. Weber, *op. cit.*, p. 185.

6. For a discussion of this problem, see the *Report of the Committee on Central Funds*, C.A. 1181, London: Church Information Board, 1956, and its evidence to justify the proposal for the strengthening of the Church Assembly Standing Committee; also the report of the committee appointed by the Archbishop of Canterbury on the administration of the Church Commissioners for England, (the *Monckton Report*), London: the Church Commissioners and the Church Information Office, 1963.

7. See the *Report of the Committee on Central Funds*, pp. 15–17, and the summary given by its chairwoman, Mrs Ridley, to the Church Assembly, in *Proceedings of Church Assembly*, vol. 36, No. 3, 1956, p. 380.

8. The differences are most marked with regard to career structures and average length of service of officials. See Thompson, *op. cit.*, especially pp. 301–03.

9. Michel Crozier, *The Bureaucratic Phenomenon*, London: Tavistock Publications, 1964, p. 3.

10. Cf. F. M. Marx, *The Administrative State*, University of Chicago Press, 1957, p. 17.

11. See Bishop Phillpotts, *A Charge Delivered to the Clergy of the Diocese of Exeter*, London: John Murray, 2nd edn. 1836, p. 33; and *The Times*, 19 February, 1845.

12. An ideal type was defined by Weber as follows: 'An ideal type is formed by the one-sided accentuation of one or more points of view and by the synthesis of a great many diffuse, discrete, more or less present and occasionally absent concrete individual phenomena, which are arranged according to those one-sidedly emphasized viewpoints into a unified analytical construct. In its conceptual purity, this mental construct cannot be found anywhere in reality' (Max Weber, *The Methodology of the Social Sciences*, trans. E. A. Shils and H. A. Finch, New York: The Free Press, 1949, p. 90).

13. The term 'metaphysical pathos' derives from the historian of ideas, Arthur O. Lovejoy, who said it was 'exemplified in any description of the nature of things, any characterization of the world to which one belongs, in terms which, like the words of a poem, evoke through their association and through a sort of empathy which they engender, a congenial mood or tone of feelings' (A. O. Lovejoy, *The Great Chain of Being*, Cambridge, Mass., 1948, p. 11). Cf. A. W. Gouldner, 'Metaphysical Pathos and the Theory of Bureaucracy', in *American Political Science Review*, 1955, pp. 496–507.

14. As a permanent body the Ecclesiastical Commissioners grew out of the Commission of Inquiry set up by Peel in 1835 'to consider the state of the Established Church with reference to Ecclesiastical Duties and Revenues'. In 1836 the first permanent Commission was appointed for the purposes of the augmentation of poorer livings and the endowment of new livings; the suspension and reorganization of capitular and episcopal estates; and the rearrangement, extension, and creation of parishes, dioceses, and other ecclesiastical districts. Parliamentary select committees reported on it in 1847–48, 1856, and 1862–63.

15. Valerie Pitt, *The Church Commissioners for England*, Prism Pamphlet No. 36, London; Prism Publications, 1967, pp. 8 and 10.

16. Paul M. Harrison has termed this 'rational-pragmatic' or 'rational-expediential' authority, as distinct from Max Weber's 'rational-legal' type of authority, which in an episcopal church would refer to the authority of the episcopate resting on a legality based on the belief in its direct institution by God. See Harrison, *op. cit.*, pp. 67–69.

17. The Bishop of Exeter, 'Centralization and Decentralization', two articles in *The Church Assembly News*, Vol. 1, Nos. 4 and 5, April–May 1924.

18. *The Church Assembly News*, Vol. 1, No. 6, June 1924.

19. See Thompson, *op.cit.*, ch. 7, for a fuller discussion of the Church Assembly departments, their structure as it relates to the bureaucratic type, and the dysfunctional behavioural characteristics.

20. Cf. F. M. Marx, *op. cit.*, p. 16.

21. See Thompson, *op. cit.*, pp. 327 ff.

22. *Parish and People*, January 1966, p. 10.

23. *Report of the Committee on Central Funds*, p. 15.

24. *Proceedings of Church Assembly*, Vol. 36, No. 3, 1956, pp. 393–96. The Archbishop of Canterbury, on this occasion, was more concerned with the defects in the organization as they obstructed effective operation, and he predicted that the proposed rationalization would have to take place eventually. (*P.C.A.*, Vol. 37, No. 2, 1957, p. 300.) Subsequent events have borne out the Archbishop's prediction, although not without opposition from those critics who can see no distinction between rationalization and bureaucratization.

25. S. N. Eisenstadt, 'Bureaucracy, Bureaucratization and Debureaucratization', in *Administrative Science Quarterly* 4, pp. 302–20.

26. A comparative analysis of different organizations in terms of the structural components of bureaucracy is being carried out by the Industrial Administration Research Unit at the University of Aston.

27. David M. Paton, Preface to the British edition of the World Council of Churches' Faith and Order Commission Report, *The Old and the New in the Church*, SCM Press, 1961, p. 8.

28. The Rt Rev. Eric Treacy in the *Church Times*, 12 February, 1965.

3 Some Aspects of the Social Geography of Religion in England: the Roman Catholics and the Mormons

John Gay

DURING the course of its development geography has greatly extended its boundaries, but the field of religion has always lain beyond them. Religion is commonly thought to lie outside the scope of empirical enquiry, and this may have deterred the geographer from ventures into what he feared would end up as metaphysics. However, it is possible to study religion within the geographic framework, and geographical method can be applied to the examination of religious institutions.[1]

This article is an attempt to sketch out a field of enquiry. It is not possible to give here a detailed rationale of the geography of religion, but it is hoped in some small way to illustrate a few of the methods which can be applied and the results which can be obtained. One of the tasks of the geographer is to discover distribution patterns and to assess the possible reasons behind the variations in distribution between one area and another. The geography of religion is a new subject in this country, and little work has been done on trying to discover the patterns of distribution. Source material is sparse, and always requires a great deal of careful analysis before it can be used with any degree of confidence.[2]

It is tempting to offer facile explanations for the distribution patterns which emerge. However, the combination of factors at work in any one area is always complex, and any conclusions drawn have to be viewed with extreme caution. In order to avoid the danger of excessive oversimplification, it is proposed to take two religious groups, the Roman Catholics and the Mormons, and to examine them in a little detail.

In Britain the three historic divisions of the country are reinforced by a similar religious differentiation. The Presbyterianism of Scotland

and the chapel nonconformity of Wales stand in sharp contrast to the religious personality of England. Different sets of historical, geographical and social circumstances have operated in each of the three countries, and so it was expedient to exclude Scotland and Wales from this study.

THE ROMAN CATHOLICS IN ENGLAND[3]

Pre-Reformation England was staunchly Roman Catholic. If we are to believe Maynard Smith,[4] the people as a whole were devout and conscientious in the performance of their religious duties. Although they rarely had a conception of the Church in its wider aspect, they were full of enthusiasm at the parochial level. The spiritual and material sides of life were so inextricably intertwined that it was impossible to separate the two. Life was unthinkable without the Roman Catholic Church.

The process of Reformation in England was set in motion by Henry VIII.[5] However, it took a long time for new ideas and ways to percolate through to the parish level, and even longer for them to gain acceptance. When Elizabeth ascended the throne in 1558, the Reformation was still external to the lives of most Englishmen. By the end of her reign, however, a Protestant Church of England was firmly established, and penal legislation was in force against those who were determined to adhere to the 'old faith' and the authority of Rome.

The first attempt to estimate the number and distribution of Roman Catholics in post-Reformation England was made by Usher[6] for the year 1603. After analysing the data available, he decided that it was impossible to calculate accurately the number of Roman Catholic laymen in England at that time, but he hazarded a guess of between three-quarters of a million and one million, which represents just under 20% of the total population. More revealing, however, are his estimates for the various districts of England and Wales (see Map 1). Roman Catholicism was still strong in the more isolated parts of the country, namely Cornwall, the Welsh Marches, Wales, and the counties north of the Mersey-Humber line. In contrast, the proportion of Roman Catholics in the total population base was low in the whole of south-east and south-central England, the northern Home Counties and East Anglia. The lowest proportions were recorded in Devonshire and the group of counties round London.

It is difficult to obtain accurate figures for the seventeenth century. It seems that numbers declined gradually during most of the century, and that the process was accelerated by the events following the Revolution of 1688, which heralded a period of eclipse for Roman Catholicism in England. By 1728 only about 5% of the population was Roman Catholic.

It is possible to assess the geographical distribution of Roman Catholics in the early eighteenth century by means of a method devised by Magee.[7] He expresses the Catholic rentals for each county, given in the registrations for 1715–20, as a percentage of the Land Tax Assessment for that county. Magee admits that this method lacks precision, owing to deficiencies in the techniques used to calculate the Land Tax Assessments. Nevertheless, it does give a helpful guide to the main features of Roman Catholic distribution at this time.

On average the Roman Catholic land values were 5% of the total Land Tax Assessments for this period. Magee divided England into two parts by a line drawn between the Bristol Channel and the Wash, with a bulge southwards to include Oxfordshire. Apart from Sussex and Hampshire, all the counties with percentages above the national average of 5% lay to the north of this line (see Map 2). The average figure for all the counties south of the line was 2·7%, while to the north it was 11%.

Not only was the contrast between the northern and southern averages so great, but the line itself represented a clear divide. The counties immediately north of it (Monmouthshire, Herefordshire, Worcestershire, Warwickshire, Oxfordshire, Northamptonshire and Lincolnshire) had an average of 7·5%, while the average of those immediately to the south of it (Gloucestershire, Wiltshire, Berkshire, Buckinghamshire, Bedfordshire, Huntingdonshire, Cambridgeshire and Norfolk) was only 3·1%. The abruptness of the dividing line is most evident towards the eastern end, where Bedfordshire, Huntingdonshire and Cambridgeshire, with an average of under 1%, stand in sharp contrast to their immediate neighbours, Rutland, Northamptonshire and Lincolnshire, whose average is 7%. Magee was convinced that this line was no vague or arbitrary boundary, but that in 1720 it presented a definite cleavage.

Catholics were least represented in the West Country, in Wales, and in the group of counties stretching south from the Wash (Cambridgeshire, Huntingdonshire, Bedfordshire and Hertfordshire). The highest percentage was in Lancashire – the chief centre of

Roman Catholicism in England from the Reformation to the present day. In the south only Sussex and Hampshire had percentages above the average, and this was largely due to the presence of certain wealthy Roman Catholic landowning families in these two counties. The only northern county which failed to exceed the 5% average was Cheshire.

A comparison between the distribution pattern of 1603 and 1720 shows the main difference to be in the south-west, where Roman Catholicism appears to have collapsed completely by 1720. The absence of wealthy aristocratic Roman Catholic families in the south-west could have been the cause of the collapse. Roman Catholicism had also died out in Wales by 1720. In the early eighteenth century, as in 1603, the greatest Roman Catholic strength lay to the north of the Humber–Mersey line.

By the middle of the eighteenth century Roman Catholicism in this country had reached its nadir. The penal legislation in the years following the Revolution had achieved its objective, and two separate counts of Roman Catholics in the late eighteenth century showed that they formed barely 1% of the total population.[8] In many places congregations had disappeared, and everywhere they had shrunk in size.

There were scarcely any Roman Catholics in the West Country or in certain of the midland counties by the end of the eighteenth century. London had the largest absolute number of Roman Catholics, but Lancashire had the highest proportion in relation to the total population. Large Roman Catholic populations were also to be found in Staffordshire and in the northern counties of Yorkshire, Durham and Northumberland. Although numbers were low in absolute terms, the proportion of Roman Catholics in relation to total population was high in Cumberland and Westmorland.

Two factors go a long way to explaining the distribution pattern of Roman Catholics at the end of the eighteenth century: first, physical isolation and distance from London, and, secondly, the influence of the gentry and nobility. Indeed, the second factor is frequently linked with the first. The northern counties of England, being a great distance from London, and containing large areas of isolated hill country, were slow to receive the ideas of the Reformation.

It was possible for farmers, yeomen and even townspeople to remain Catholic in the northern counties, but elsewhere the continuance of the Roman faith was dependent upon the existence of a Catholic family of squires. In most parts of late-sixteenth-century England the feudal relationship still operated, and if an aristocratic or landowning family was Roman Catholic, it would support a priest and enable a Roman Catholic community to centre on the 'great house'. The policy of allowing recusant peers and gentry to practise their faith, adopted under Elizabeth I, was continued under the Stuarts.

Under the patronage of a Roman Catholic squire or nobleman a small pocket of Roman Catholicism could flourish. The squire would build a chapel in his house and would support a priest, without whom the administration of the sacraments and hence the practice of Catholicism would be impossible. The feudal relationship ensured that most of the squire's tenants and retainers would be Catholic, and would enjoy the protection of their patron.

It was one thing to pass penal measures against the Catholics; it was another to enforce them. The government depended upon the local gentry, acting as Justices of the Peace, to administer the laws. In the south and east, where Roman Catholics were weak and had few representatives on the local benches, the penal laws were enforced with some rigour; but where Roman Catholicism was stronger, as in the Midlands, the Welsh Marches and the north, there was usually a sufficient number of Catholic Justices to ensure that the penal laws had little practical effect. This process heightened the contrast between areas, as it further weakened Catholicism in places where the Catholics were already in a small minority, and allowed a strengthening in places where Catholicism was firmly established.

The dependence of Catholicism for its survival on the great land-owning families had its drawbacks. If a squire abandoned the 'old faith' and became Protestant, then the chapel would be closed, the priest dismissed, and a whole Catholic community would disintegrate. During the latter half of the seventeenth century and throughout the eighteenth century many of the great Catholic families turned Protestant, and others became extinct. So Catholicism in England became inextricably linked with the Catholic squires and nobility. If we could plot the distribution map of all the Catholic county families in eighteenth-century England, we should have a good distribution map of Catholicism. Thus we find the relative strength of Catholicism in eighteenth-century Sussex and Hampshire to be due to the existence of several wealthy Catholic families in these two counties. This relationship between the Catholic Church and the landowning gentry was the hallmark of English Catholicism up to the early years of the nineteenth century, and even today traces of it can still be discerned.

The first signs of the Catholic dawn in this country were the Relief Acts of 1778 and 1779. During the following fifty years the restrictions on Catholics were gradually lifted, and the Emancipation Bill of 1829 finally ended all their legal disabilities. The nineteenth century saw two strands emerge within English Catholicism: the older English Catholics and the Irish Catholics.[9]

The older English Catholics

The preservation of Catholicism in England from the time of the Reformation through to the nineteenth century lay in the hands of the Catholic aristocracy. The largest number of Catholic estates was to be found in Northumberland, Durham and the farming areas of Lancashire, especially in the Fylde. There were further areas of Catholicism in Yorkshire, particularly in the North Riding, and also isolated pockets throughout the Midlands. Relatively few Catholic estates were to be found in the south and south-west or in East Anglia, and, even where the occupants of the 'great house' had remained Roman Catholic, there was often little loyalty on the part of the tenants and workers. The Catholic village unit had less chance of peaceful coexistence in the more hostile southern environment where the penal laws were more stringently applied.

An accelerating movement from the land to the new industrial areas took place in the nineteenth century, and it was natural that some of these new industrial workers should have originated from the rural estates of Catholic landowners. In Lancashire a considerable exodus took place from estates in the Fylde into Preston and then on south to Chorley and Liverpool. Similarly the new industrial ventures of Northumberland and Durham were able to draw on a long-established Catholic rural population. A strong sense of group solidarity meant that Catholic entrepreneurs would employ their co-religionists wherever possible.

Historically the Catholic rural population has been small and almost entirely centred upon the estates of the Catholic aristocracy and landowners. Normally Catholics were allowed to remain unmolested provided they stepped out of the main stream of national life and were content with life on their country estates. It is small wonder that by the nineteenth century they had become noticeably detached and unconcerned about current political and social problems. They were well assimilated into local life, but beyond this they did not venture.

The immigration of Irish Catholics into this country in the nineteenth century was not welcomed by the old-established English Catholics. There was little in common between the Roman Catholic upper class and their brethren of Irish descent, and the lack of a Roman Catholic middle class further emphasized the gulf between the two groups.

The Irish Catholics in England[10]

By the end of the eighteenth century the traditional mistrust and suspicion with which the English Catholics had to contend was fast disappearing. But just as English Roman Catholicism was beginning to be recognized *de facto*, a new element, in the form of the Irish Catholics, appeared on the scene. This had the effect of reversing the process of recognition and again Catholicism began to be viewed as a threat.

The pivotal point in the history of Irish immigration into England was the potato famine of 1845–49; but the origins date back much earlier, to the closing years of the eighteenth century, with the onset of the Industrial Revolution and the consequent demand for cheap industrial labour. Already by 1841 there were nearly 300,000 Irish-born residents in England and Wales, representing 1·9% of the total population. The potato famine had the effect of greatly accelerating a process which was already in operation. By a fortunate coincidence, at the same time as Irish economic conditions favoured emigration, the English economy was only too anxious to receive the immigrants. Unskilled labour was required in great quantity for the construction of docks, railways and industrial plants, and the English were delighted to hand this work over to their Irish neighbours.

The large majority of the immigrants landed at Liverpool. From there they moved in search of work into South Lancashire, Leeds and the north-east, and along the railway construction lines. Between 1841 and 1861 the number of Irish-born in England and Wales increased from 300,000 to 600,000, and by 1861 they accounted for 3% of the total population base. Most of them, before leaving Ireland, had been engaged in agriculture. On arrival in England they found that the only work available was unskilled labouring in the great industrial cities. Most of the Irish settled in our large new urban complexes, and each new arrival of immigrants made for the growing centres of industry where employment would be available. The Census of 1861 found the majority of Irish-born immigrants in Lancashire, Cheshire, Metropolitan London, Yorkshire, Durham and Northumberland, and more particularly in big towns such as Liverpool, London, Manchester, Leeds, Bradford, Sheffield, Newcastle and Birmingham. It was the Irish immigrants who made Roman Catholicism in England an urban phenomenon.

Late-nineteenth-century Catholicism was largely an Irish affair. Writing in 1887, Cardinal Manning said that he had spent his life working for the Irish occupation of England. He estimated that 80% of the Roman Catholics in England at that time were Irish, and, of the remainder, the majority were in sympathy with Ireland. Unfortunately, the national census of population is of only limited value in determining the size of the Irish community in any one place. The number of Irish-*born* people is recorded, but not the number of people born in England of Irish parents. It is therefore impossible to determine the number of second-generation Irish immigrants.

It is possible to think of the nineteenth-century Irish Catholics as forming an ethnic church in this country. Socially and culturally distinct from the older English Catholics, the Irish quickly dominated and swamped English Catholicism. An ethnic church is characterized geographically by the 'ghetto concept'. The sense of being aliens in a foreign land causes immigrants to group together, and the religious institution, transplanted from the homeland, forms a focus of community life. The Irish found themselves assigned to the lowest strata of English society and they clustered in the 'twilight zones' of our coke towns. The Catholic Church became the main link between them and their native Ireland.

The Irish in England are still conscious of being a distinctive group and the process of assimilation is far from complete.[11] We still find recognizable areas of Irish Catholic settlement in particular quarters of our cities, and although increasing upward social mobility and the resultant move to the suburbs has broken their former rigidity, they still form recognizable geographical units.

In recent years the Irish-born population in England has increased sharply. These increases have been most marked in the London

Metropolitan area and in the Midlands, while the numbers in Lancashire have only increased slightly. The six major conurbations (Greater London, West Midlands, Merseyside, South-east York-shire, West Yorkshire and Tyneside) account for over half the Irish-born population in this country. Not all the Irish, however, make for the conurbations. With the diversification of industry and the spread of light industry to small centres, some of the Irish have made for these new areas. The Midlands and Greater London rather than Lancashire are the expanding areas of today, and it is to these that the Irish come. The majority of Irish still find employment in unskilled labouring, but an increasing number are entering the skilled and professional occupational groups. This increase in social status produces geographical mobility in the form of a movement out of the old Catholic 'ghetto areas'.

The 1851 Census

We have to wait until 1851 before we can obtain a detailed picture of Roman Catholic distribution, and in that year, for the first and last time, a section on religion was included in the national census of population.[12] Despite its many deficiencies, the Report on Religious Worship provides us with source material of sufficient accuracy to enable us to build up a map of the geographical distribution of Roman Catholicism in England.

The Census was carried out on Sunday, 30 March 1851, and one of its aims was to count the number of attendances at the morning, the afternoon and the evening services. These were listed in three separate columns with the total attendances for the whole day given in a fourth. No attempt was made to discover how many people attended more than one service on that day.

In order to make these figures geographically meaningful it was necessary to relate them to population totals. Inglis's method of summing the morning, afternoon and evening attendances and then expressing this total as a percentage of the total population was used,[13] and the resultant percentage is referred to as the Index of Attendance (I. of A.). It must be noted, however, that the I. of A. will be appreciably higher than the percentage of actual people attending, for some people would have been to more than one service.

The I. of A. is of great value to the geographer, as it enables him to compare one area with another. The Report on Religious Worship lists the attendance figures for each Poor Law Union or Registration

District by religious denomination. It was considered that the figures were too inaccurate at this level for general use in geographical comparison, and so their use was restricted to the county level. In the cases of Lancashire, Cheshire, Northumberland and Durham, however, a method was devised partially to eliminate the errors at the Registration District level so that they could be used for a more detailed study.[14]

Catholics in Lancashire and Cheshire in 1851

Map 3 gives the distribution of Roman Catholic practice in Lancashire and Cheshire for 1851. A line running north-east from Chester separates the two communities into a Protestant east and a Catholic west. With the one exception of the area in the immediate neighbourhood of Manchester, the districts of high Catholic practice all lay to the west and north of this line. The highest proportions of Catholics were in the three northern districts of Fylde, Garstang and Clitheroe – the home of the old-established rural population based on the estates of the great Catholic landowning families.

By 1851 the growth of Catholicism in Lancashire was the result of twin forces: the southward drift of agricultural workers from the Catholic estates in north Lancashire to the new areas of industry and the fanwise movement out from Liverpool of Irish immigrants. Both these movements are apparent from the map.

Compared with Lancashire the incidence of Roman Catholicism in Cheshire was low. Over the whole of central and south Cheshire a small Catholic rural population registered a practice well below the national average. Catholics were numerous on the Wirral, an overspill area for Liverpool, and there were above average attendances in the four districts to the south and south-east of Manchester, and also in the industrial district of Runcorn.

Catholics in the North-east in 1851

A sizeable Catholic rural population was to be found on the Catholic estates in Northumberland and Durham. The presence of Catholics in purely rural Registration Districts (see Map 4) attests to this. The highest I.s of A., however, were around Newcastle, Gateshead and Durham and also in the extreme south-east around the Hartlepools and Middlesbrough. These were the main centres of industry in the north-east and so attracted large numbers of Irish immigrants, who were reinforced by Catholics moving off the rural estates in the north-east.

Catholics in England in 1851

Map 5 shows the geographical variation in attendance by county on Census Sunday, 1851. With the exception of the London Metropolitan area, Catholics were few in number everywhere south of a line from Bristol to Grimsby, that is, in the West Country, the East Midlands, East Anglia and the whole of the south of England. Lancashire stood out as the county with the largest population of Roman Catholics, followed by two groups of counties: Durham, Northumberland and the North Riding in the north-east; and a belt running from Cheshire through Staffordshire to Warwickshire.

We are able to make certain comparisons and contrasts between the geographical distributions in 1851 and those of 1720. By 1851 Catholicism had virtually died out on the Welsh Border, in Westmorland and along the southern limit of the 'Catholic North', that is, in Oxfordshire, Northamptonshire, Rutland and Lincolnshire. Catholic influence had increased greatly in Cheshire and London by 1851, largely as a result of Irish immigration. Otherwise the dichotomy between the Catholic North and the non-Catholic South remained intact.

Catholicism in England in 1962[15]

It has been possible to compile a map of the density of the practising Roman Catholic community in England for the year 1962 by relating the statistics for Mass attendance[16] to the total population (see Map 6). Four areas of high density stand out:

1. The North – Cumberland, Northumberland, Durham and the North Riding
2. Lancashire and Cheshire
3. Warwickshire
4. London and Middlesex

Intermediate densities are found in the West Riding and in a large area to the north and east of London. Densities are lowest in Westmorland, the Welsh Border counties of Herefordshire, Shropshire and Worcestershire, the West Country and a large block of counties adjacent to the Wash.

A direct comparison between the I. of A. for 1851 and the percentage of Mass attenders for 1962 is not possible, but the overall variations in the distribution pattern can be compared. Westmorland stood out as an area with a small percentage of Catholics both in 1851 and 1962. The belt of strong Roman Catholic practice which ran from Lancashire to Warwickshire in 1851 had been broken by 1962. It appears that Roman Catholic strength in Staffordshire had not grown at the same rate as in Cheshire and Warwickshire. The four northern counties of Cumberland, Northumberland, Durham and the North Riding have remained Catholic strongholds over the last hundred years, and Lancashire has always been in a category of its own, having the highest proportion of Roman Catholics to the total population in England.

The most significant change in the distribution pattern has been the relative growth of Catholicism in the whole area within a radius of sixty miles of the centre of London. In 1851 it was only the County of London which stood out amid the general sea of low density. By 1962 this had been drastically altered. Middlesex had joined the County of London as an area of high density, and a whole group of counties around London had medium densities.

What then had caused this growth of Catholicism in the south-east? Admittedly there has been a general movement of population into the south-east, but this, in itself, would not account for the increase in the proportion of Roman Catholics in the south-east. It is possible to discern three processes at work. The first is simply immigration from Catholic countries overseas. Secondly, in recent years the Catholic population has been increasing in wealth, with the result of a greater Catholic representation in the middle classes. This upward social movement produces geographical mobility and a movement out of the Catholic 'ghetto areas'. London tends to act as a magnet to the upward spiralists. Finally, Catholics have always in the past been under-represented in the London region, and the differential growth rate we are now witnessing can be seen in terms of a stabilizing process. The deterrents to an overt practice of Catholicism which operated from the time of the Reformation onwards were gradually lifted during the nineteenth century, although the social deterrents persisted well into the twentieth. These deterrents had been felt most markedly in the south-east of England.

The future trends in the geographical distribution of Catholicism are likely to be towards a more even spread over the country. Increasing assimilation and social mobility are breaking down the old ghetto areas, and the Catholic authorities are making great efforts to deal with the problem of rural Catholicism.[17] In years to come the geographical distribution of Catholicism in England is likely to resemble more closely the distribution pattern of the population as a whole.

THE CHURCH OF JESUS CHRIST OF LATTER DAY SAINTS[18]

The history of the Mormon Church began in the early 1820s in the United States of America when the founder of the movement, a certain Joseph Smith, claimed to have two visions from God.[19] During the next twenty years the Mormon Church grew in numbers and strength, despite encountering severe opposition and persecution. The Mormons were forced to leave their original settlements in Illinois and travelled west to Utah under their new leader, Brigham Young, where they founded Salt Lake City.

The Mormons first appeared on the English religious kaleido-scope in 1837, when seven Mormon missionaries landed at Liverpool. From here they made their way north to Preston, where they received an enthusiastic welcome and baptized their first converts in the waters of the Ribble.

The Mormons in 1851

By the time of the 1851 Religious Census[20] Mormon activity had spread over large parts of England. The Census itself must be used with considerable caution when attempting to assess the geographical distribution of Mormons. In spite of its faults, however, it enables the geographer to plot the general pattern of a real variation in Mormon strength.

There was a total of about 35,000 attendances at Mormon places of worship in England on Census Sunday; but, as some would attend more than one service a day, it is unlikely that the 35,000 attendances would represent 35,000 actual persons. An estimate of between 25,000 and 30,000 people attending Mormon services on Census Sunday is hazarded. This is not to imply that all those attending were fully professed members. We have no means of assessing how many were members, and it would be a fruitless task to guess.

Absolute numbers tell us very little; they need to be related to the total population base. This has been achieved by expressing the number of Mormon attendances per thousand of the population on a county basis. Over England as a whole, the Mormon attendances were two per thousand, and the regional variations are shown on Map 7.

The Mormons in England looked to the New World as the source of their religion and for a supply of early missionaries. There was also a considerable desire on the part of the early converts to emigrate to America and make their way to the Promised Land of Utah and the temple in Salt Lake City. It was inevitable, therefore, that those English ports which maintained regular services to and from the eastern seaboard of America should become centres of Mormon activity. Bristol, Southampton and Liverpool became focal points linking the English Mormons with their prophets in the States. The high incidence of Mormonism in Gloucestershire and Hampshire is clearly seen on the map, although the large number of Mormons in Liverpool did not have much effect on the general total for Lancashire.

We can also trace lines of Mormon penetration out from these three centres. From Southampton they spread over Hampshire and north-west into the surrounding counties of Dorsetshire, Wiltshire and Somersetshire. Similarly, influences filtered south from Bristol into the same three counties, as well as travelling along a south-west/ north-east axis through Gloucestershire, Warwickshire and Leicester- shire into Nottinghamshire. The importance of Liverpool's link with the New World is reflected in Mormon presence in Lancashire, Cheshire and the West Riding.

Taking the total number of attendances, we find that nearly 75% of the total is made up by the following counties or groups of counties:

1. Lancashire (11·6), Cheshire (5·2), West Riding (7·2)   24%
2. Dorset (2·2), Somerset (2·5), Wiltshire (2·8),
   Hampshire (8·7), Gloucestershire (7·3)   23·5%
3. Metropolitan London   12·8%
4. Warwickshire   7·5%
5. Nottinghamshire   5·7%

Mormonism was, however, a relatively new phenomenon in this country in 1851, and it had not spread into the extremities of England. Thus there were no Mormon attendances registered in Cornwall, and the five northern counties of Cumberland, Westmorland, the North Riding, Northumberland and Durham only accounted for 1·9% of the total Mormon attendances in England. Similarly, in the south-eastern counties of Suffolk, Essex, Surrey, Kent and Sussex attendances were low.

The 1851 map reflects the pattern of an organization very much in its infancy. It was only just beginning to spread out from the ports of arrival into their immediate hinterlands. It is interesting that Mormon missionaries had already achieved successes in Metropolitan London. This is an obvious place to begin an evangelizing campaign on account of its key position and its unique role in the country. They had also been successful in the northern Home Counties. It appears that the environment of these counties (Hertfordshire, Bedfordshire, Huntingdonshire, Cambridgeshire and Northampton-shire) is conducive to all types and persuasions of religious groups.[21]

The Mormons in 1967

The whole pattern and ethos of the Mormon Church has altered considerably since 1851. In many respects its organization is modelled on lines formulated by American big business, and its missionaries are fully trained in salesmanship technique. An air of professional competence is exuded. The average Englishman, brought up amid the historic pageantry of his religious institutions, usually finds the Mormon approach difficult to comprehend. But undoubtedly the Mormon appeal is novel and is likely to succeed with many.

It is possible to build up a picture of Mormon activity and strength in this country today by using their membership figures and also from information concerning their church buildings.[22] A member of the Mormon Church is a person who has received a Mormon baptism. Most members are made by conversion during the teenage or adult period of life. The presence of American airmen resident in England who are Mormons and are included in the English totals is likely to distort the true pattern somewhat. Little can be done about this, however, as the method of enumeration used by the Mormons fails to distinguish between nationalities.

The distribution of Mormon members over the country (see Map 8) forms a distinctive pattern. The four ports which have or had close links with the USA (Bristol, Southampton, Liverpool and Plymouth) each have a large Mormon following among their populations. Another port, Hull, also has a surprisingly large Mormon congregation.

Mormon strength lies in the northern half of England. Taking two of the traditional dividing lines, we find that about 60% of Mormon membership is north of a line from the Severn to the Wash, and 45% north of a line between the Dee and the Humber. More specifically, a large proportion of the northern total is found in the three stake[23] areas of Manchester, Leeds and Sunderland.

The Mormons have met with little success in London, the south-east and right along the south coast from Kent to Cornwall (Southampton and Plymouth excepted). Congregations are to be found in these areas, but relative to the total population, membership is very low. The map of Mormon church building (Map 9) confirms the general features of geographical distribution as outlined above.

What does the future hold for Mormons in this country? Their missionary effectiveness is rapidly increasing and already they have a missionary force of nearly a thousand young volunteers operating in England. The Mormons present a united front, as their authoritarian structure has prevented any serious theological dissensions from developing within the Church. It is difficult to see how the Mormons in this country can do anything but increase in numbers in the years which lie ahead. Whether they can modify their approach in order to appeal to the Southerner remains to be seen.

CONCLUSIONS

It is hoped that these two studies of the Roman Catholics and the Mormons in England have illustrated some of the ways in which a geographer can approach the subject of religion, and some of the results which can be obtained. The studies are indicative rather than exhaustive of the subject. Inevitably they have concentrated on historical depth, for it is only in this way that long-term trends and processes can be observed. The 1851 Census provides the geographer with an excellent backcloth against which to set the present pattern of a real variation. The geographer of religion has to understand the processes which operated in the past, and then he is in a position to assess contemporary distribution patterns.

NOTES

1. The following provide good examples of the geographical study of religion: F. Boulard, *An Introduction to Religious Sociology*, London: Darton, Longman and Todd, 1960; W. A. Hotchkiss, *Areal Patterns of Religious Institutions in*

Cincinnati (University of Chicago Department of Geography, Research Paper 13), Chicago, 1950; E. James, *A Social Geography of Belfast*, London: Oxford University Press, 1960; *Annals of the Association of American Geographers*, Albany, 1961, pp. 139–93; W. Zelinsky, *An Approach to the Religious Geography of the United States: Patterns of Church Membership in 1952*.

2. An instance of general conclusions based on shaky evidence is provided by the section on 'The Strength of Religion' in *The Reader's Digest Complete Atlas of the British Isles*, London, 1965, pp. 120 f. The maps, purporting to show the strength of each major denomination, were based on the Registrar General's Statistics of Marriages by Religious Denomination. The number of marriages conducted under the auspices of a particular denomination does not provide a clear indication of the overall strength of that denomination.

3. Occasionally figures and information on Wales have been included, but this is only incidental, and no attempt is made to discuss Catholicism in Wales.

4. H. M. Smith, *Pre-Reformation England*, London: Macmillan 1938.

5. For a full account of the Reformation see O. Chadwick, *The Reformation*, London: Penguin Books, 1964.

6. R. G. Usher, *The Reconstruction of the English Church*, 2 vols., New York and London: Appleton, 1910.

7. B. Magee, *The English Recusants*, London: Burns & Oates, 1938.

8. J. Berington, *The State and Behaviour of English Catholics from the Reformation to the Year 1780*, London: 1780.

9. For general reference see G. A. Beck (editor), *The English Catholics 1850–1950*, London: Burns & Oates, 1950, and E. I. Watkin, *Roman Catholicism in England from the Reformation to 1950*, London: Oxford University Press, 1957.

10. Detailed accounts can be consulted in J. V. Hickey, *The Irish Rural Immigrant and British Urban Society*, London: Newman Demographic Survey, 1960, and J. A. Jackson, *The Irish in Britain*, London: Routledge and Kegan Paul, 1963.

11. C. K. Ward, *Priests and People*, Liverpool: Liverpool University Press, 1961. An excellent account of a parish in Liverpool.

12. Census of Great Britain 1851: *Religious Worship in England and Wales*, London, 1853.

13. K. S. Inglis, *Churches and the Working Classes in Victorian England*, London: Routledge and Kegan Paul, 1963.

14. The method consisted of estimating the attendance figures for the defective returns, drawing on whatever other information was available.

15. I am greatly indebted to Mr A. E. C. W. Spencer of Cavendish Square College, London, W.1, for all the information he made available to me. The two following reports, both by him, are unpublished: *The Demography and Sociography of the Catholic Community of England and Wales*, 1965; and *Statistical Definitions of Belonging to the Church*, 1962.

16. The statistics were collected by the Newman Demographic Survey.

17. The problem in many rural areas is that Catholics are frequently many miles away from the nearest church, and are unable to receive the sacraments essential for the practice of their faith.

18. This is the official title, although they are normally referred to as the Mormons. The term 'saint' is used in the original sense of a follower of Christ, and is not meant to imply canonization.

19. For further details of Mormon history and theology see R. R. Mullen, *The Mormons*, London: W. H. Allen, 1967. This is a very readable account written by a non-Mormon.

20. See n. 12 above.

21. A conclusion drawn from the author's research work, as yet unpublished.

22. I am greatly indebted to the various officials of the Mormon Church in this country who made this information available. They could not have been more helpful and explicit in dealing with my queries.

23. The Mormons divide England into five independent Missions. However, there are four 'stake areas' (the three named here and London) which operate as separate units, although they are geographically inside Mission areas.

MAPS

Roman Catholics and Mormons

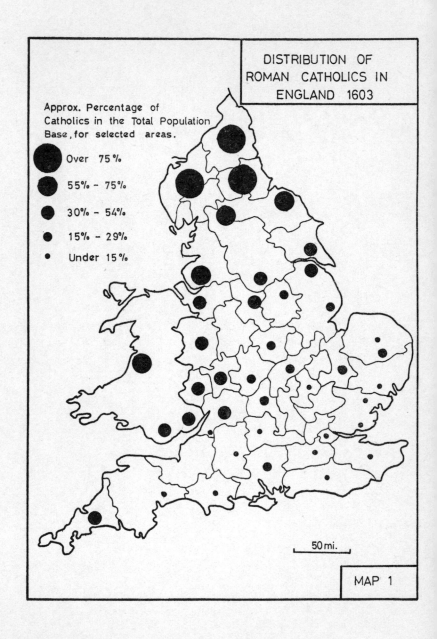

DISTRIBUTION OF
ROMAN CATHOLICS IN
ENGLAND 1603

Approx. Percentage of
Catholics in the Total Population
Base, for selected areas.

Over 75%

55% - 75%

30% - 54%

15% - 29%

Under 15%

50 mi.

MAP 1

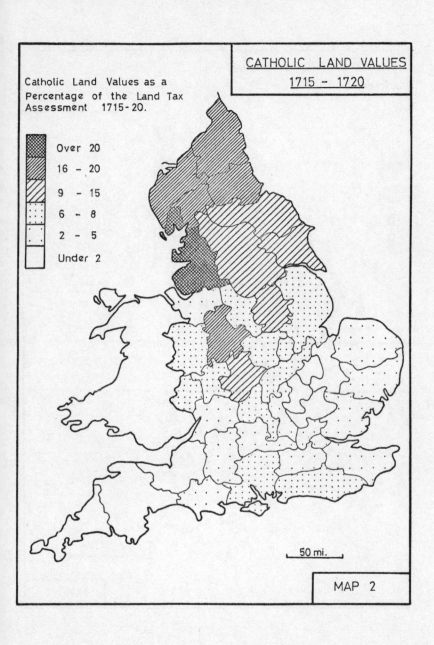

Catholic Land Values as a
Percentage of the Land Tax
Assessment 1715-20.

CATHOLIC LAND VALUES
1715 - 1720

Over 20
16 - 20
9 - 15
6 - 8
2 - 5
Under 2

50 mi.

MAP 2

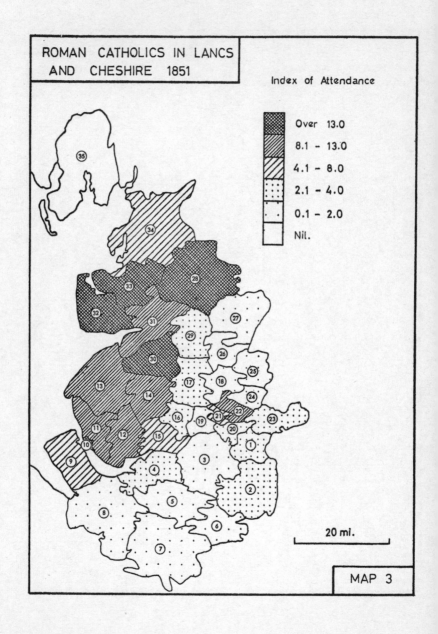

ROMAN CATHOLICS IN LANCS
AND CHESHIRE 1851

Index of Attendance

Over 13.0
8.1 - 13.0
4.1 - 8.0
2.1 - 4.0
0.1 - 2.0
Nil.

20 mi.

MAP 3

REGISTRATION DISTRICTS OR POOR LAW UNIONS

1	Stockport	19	Barton-upon-Irwell
2	Macclesfield	20	Chorlton
3	Altrincham	21	Salford
4	Runcorn	22	Manchester
5	Northwich	23	Ashton-under-Lyne
6	Congleton	24	Oldham
7	Nantwich	25	Rochdale
8	Great Broughton	26	Haslingden
9	Wirral	27	Burnley
10	Liverpool	28	Clitheroe
11	West Derby	29	Blackburn
12	Prescot	30	Chorley
13	Ormskirk	31	Preston
14	Wigan	32	Fylde
15	Warrington	33	Garstang
16	Leigh	34	Lancaster
17	Bolton	35	Ulverston
18	Bury		

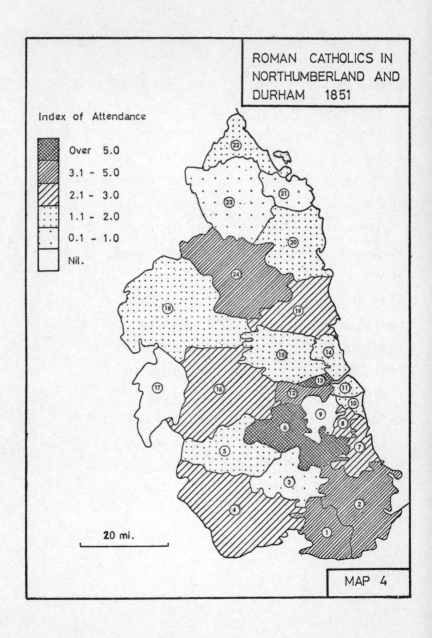

ROMAN CATHOLICS IN
NORTHUMBERLAND AND
DURHAM   1851

Index of Attendance

Over 5.0
3.1 - 5.0
2.1 - 3.0
1.1 - 2.0
0.1 - 1.0
Nil.

20 mi.

MAP 4

REGISTRATION DISTRICTS OR POOR LAW UNIONS

1	Darlington	13	Newcastle
2	Stockton	14	Tynemouth
3	Auckland	15	Castle Ward
4	Teesdale	16	Hexham
5	Weardale	17	Haltwhistle
6	Durham	18	Bellingham
7	Easington	19	Morpeth
8	Houghton-le-Spring	20	Alnwick
9	Chester-le-Street	21	Belford
10	Sunderland	22	Berwick-on-Tweed
11	South Shields	23	Glendale
12	Gateshead	24	Rothbury

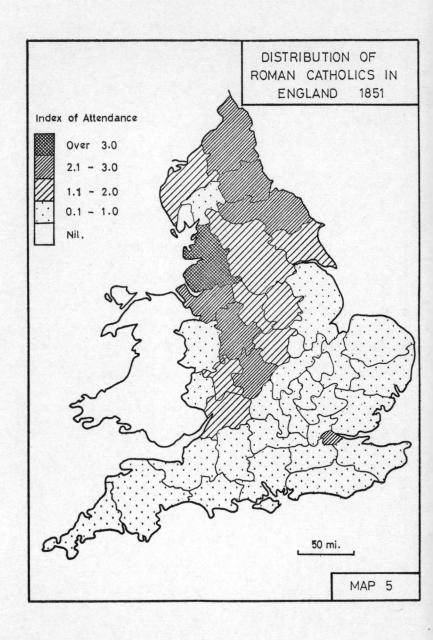

Index of Attendance

Over 3.0
2.1 – 3.0
1.1 – 2.0
0.1 – 1.0
Nil.

DISTRIBUTION OF
ROMAN CATHOLICS IN
ENGLAND 1851

50 mi.

MAP 5

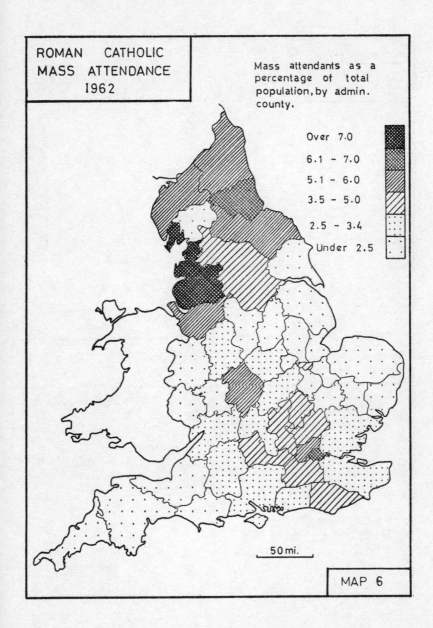

ROMAN CATHOLIC
MASS ATTENDANCE
1962

Mass attendants as a
percentage of total
population, by admin.
county.

Over 7·0
6·1 - 7·0
5·1 - 6·0
3·5 - 5·0
2·5 - 3·4
Under 2·5

50 mi.

MAP 6

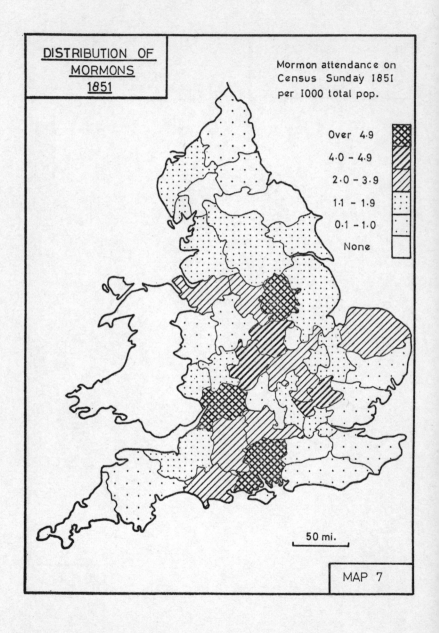

DISTRIBUTION OF
MORMONS
1851

Mormon attendance on
Census Sunday 1851
per 1000 total pop.

Over 4·9
4·0 − 4·9
2·0 − 3·9
1·1 − 1·9
0·1 − 1·0
None

50 mi.

MAP 7

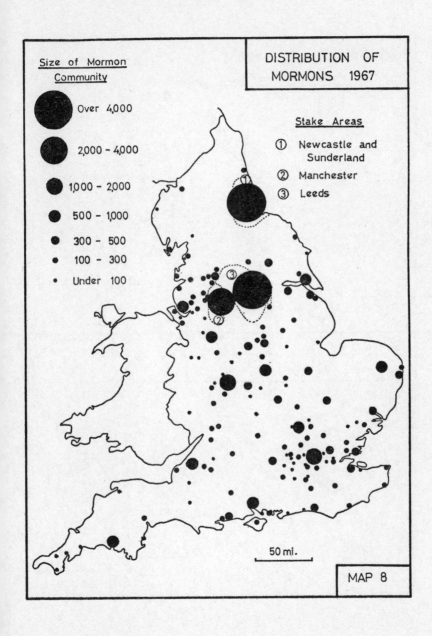

Size of Mormon
Community

● Over 4,000

● 2,000 – 4,000

● 1,000 – 2,000

● 500 – 1,000

● 300 – 500

• 100 – 300

· Under 100

DISTRIBUTION OF
MORMONS 1967

Stake Areas

① Newcastle and
Sunderland

② Manchester

③ Leeds

50 mi.

MAP 8

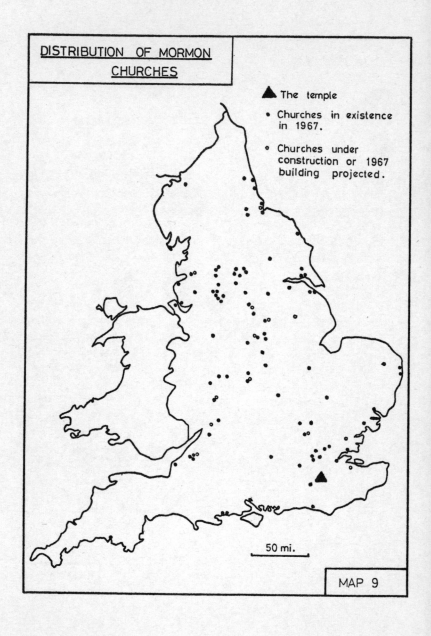

DISTRIBUTION OF MORMON CHURCHES

▲ The temple

• Churches in existence in 1967.

◦ Churches under construction or 1967 building projected.

50 mi.

MAP 9

4 Religion – a Leisure-time Pursuit?

William Pickering

I

INSTITUTIONAL religion is no longer the force in western society that it was a hundred years ago: it is certainly no longer the force that it was in the Middle Ages. In England at the present time, as well as in many other European countries, only a small fraction of the population worships Sunday by Sunday, and perhaps even fewer subscribe to all the articles of faith officially propounded by the churches. The shrunken state of religion is an uncontestable fact. The fact gives rise to a number of questions. For the sociologist, and perhaps the historian, one such question is whether the shrunken state of religion has not only meant a scaling down of the following of the churches or the withdrawal of the influence of religion within other social institutions, but a shift in the social quality of religion as it appears in society. Many observers are inclined to take such a stand (though they might not subscribe to the phrase social quality) and hold that the shrinking of religion has been accompanied by a number of profound changes. Bryan Wilson in his recent book *Religion in Secular Society* goes so far as to suggest that religion today is to be found mainly in the sects.[1] For some, his position is difficult to accept since he implies that only religion of a certain kind is in the end religion. But his general point is to be supported, namely, that there has been a shift in the nature of institutional religion with the passing of years. Those who wrestle with analysing the social quality of contemporary religion find it by no means easy to bring out its essential characteristics. That they look elsewhere to find a parallel is in itself a significant fact. Religion itself does not provide the touchstone: rather, religion is to be likened to some other form of social activity. One such activity to which it can be compared is that associated with leisure.

II

The word leisure implies freedom from involvement in what is necessary for existence. More particularly it means 'freedom from activities centering around the making of a livelihood'.[2] Modern man is encouraged to see his life divided into two types of activities – those which relate to his work and those which relate to his non-work, that is, his leisure. The former activities are held to be of prime importance since they are concerned with making a livelihood and the latter are seen to be secondary, although in these days greater importance is given to them for they are held to be of necessity complementary to occupational activities. Within the general category of leisure-time activities – and it is basically an omnibus term – are those associated with home and family life, which for the wife and mother of children are very far from 'leisure-time'. Included also in this general category are hobbies, sports, and 'just being at home'. All activity that does not involve regular financial reward can be viewed as leisure-time activity. Such a definition allows a fairly precise line to be drawn between leisure and work, but it does not avoid the problem of dealing with the multiplicity of leisure-time activites, and more especially those which are on the borderline, such as the duties of the housewife.

What is more important for our purposes is not precise definition but certain basic qualities or characteristics which are associated with leisure-time pursuits. The quest is close to establishing an 'ideal type' in the sense that Max Weber developed 'ideal types'. A person engaged in leisure-time pursuits participates in activities which are very largely open to personal choice, though such choice is limited by immediate facilities and is constrained by the age and sex of the person concerned. Leisure-time not only means freedom from work but freedom to do one of a number of activities. Further, the kind of activity that is designated leisure-time has also associated with it the notions of pleasure, recreation, or relaxation. It can be viewed as a relief from the pressures of work and an opportunity for rest and refreshment. In addition, it may lead to creative results, as in the case of some hobby. But the keynote of leisure is that the overall effect is pleasure-giving. If this be granted, then it would not be absurd to suggest that by and large people follow that form of activity which gives them most pleasure and relaxation. Indeed, a man would be looked upon as being 'irrational' or a fool if he adopted or persisted in a leisure-time activity which gave him suffering and misery, devoid of any accountable reward. For a person to have adopted some new form of leisure-time pursuit means that he has changed to something that he considers is more pleasurable or worthwhile.

III

From its earliest days the Church's attitudes towards leisure and relaxation have been ambivalent. Briefly it can be said that gross pleasures, such as debauchery and drunken brawls, were condemned as being unworthy of Christian behaviour. At the same time hard work and a respect for civil authorities, even for slaves to honour their master, were enjoined. On the other hand, by reason of the Judaic background of Christianity, some leisure-time – cessation from labour on the Sabbath or Sunday – was assumed or called for. During non-work periods Christians were expected to behave soberly and in accordance with the customs of the day where those were compatible with Christian morality. Followers were exhorted to attend the Church's corporate worship and to perform good works where there was need. Apart from the moral aspects of work and leisure, it seems reasonable to assume that Church leaders were aware of the fact that periods of leisure-time were essential for the development of the Church and for its continued existence. Assuredly, the Church could and did function during 'working hours' but its strength and growth were fostered at times when work was not the order of the day. It is quite clear that much Christian activity occurred on the Sabbath or Sunday.

At the time of the early Church, and for the centuries that followed, Christianity and indeed any religion was taken with great seriousness. The premises of religion called for such an approach. It was after all concerned with the eternal, with heaven and damnation, with life and death, with joy and suffering. It attempted to give meaning to the ultimate nature of life and to be instrumental in leading individuals to final bliss. The reality with which religion dealt suggests that religion in itself could not be taken lightly or be the subject of mockery and jest. Logically a person had to be identified with it or else deny its very foundations.

To the Christian and to members of other religions, religious activity was not viewed as a pleasurable pursuit to be compared in

nature with such activities as sports and dancing, though in cases
these were part of religious rituals. Pleasant though some of the
side effects might be for those who practised religion – and early
Christians spoke of the joy of their faith – religion was looked upon
as a matter of ultimate importance. To be a Christian in the early
Church meant in many instances undergoing a long period of
instruction in the catechumenate. Martyrdom, often by very cruel
means, was a possibility most of the early Christians had to face.
These and other characteristics were sufficient to prevent religion
being viewed as a leisure-time pursuit.

It is out of the question in a paper of this kind to examine the
Church at various periods of its history in order to establish its basic
attitudes towards leisure and towards religion. Suffice it to say that
all down the ages the Church or churches have been generally opposed to over-much leisure and that the monastic way of life was
often embraced as a reaction against a leisure-seeking society.
While some leisure was thought to be necessary, work rather than
leisure was held to be the better bed-fellow for religion. Religion was
taken seriously and most people assented to being religious – the
quarrel was over the form religion should take for society or for the
individual. To be Catholic or Protestant? To join a monastery or
remain 'in the world'?

Radical changes became apparent in the nineteenth century,
particularly towards its close. Glimpses of the changes and often
their origins can be seen in previous eras, but the nineteenth century
is critical for studying the problem under consideration. By this
time freedom to worship in any denomination had been secured.
To belong to a church, no matter what its doctrine, involved no
threat of persecution by the state. Again, not to belong to a church
entailed no handicaps relating to job-opportunities, nor did church
membership or a lack of it mean penalties against a man's family
or his property. Thus it was that certainly by the last quarter of the
century church-goers and non-church-goers had equal status in the
eyes of the law and were protected by the state as ordinary citizens.
That this had come about implied that to belong to a church, Established or Nonconformist, was to belong to a voluntary society,
that is, a society with which it is not legally necessary for an individual
to be associated. Where institutional religion is given the status of
being voluntary rather than being established the implication is that
society has officially adopted a secular position and has refused to

align itself or identify itself with a particular religion or denomination. Religion is therefore on the open market; free from state support, but free from state persecution.

Nineteenth-century Nonconformists welcomed such changes in the status of religion – indeed it was they who helped foster them. England had accepted the Nonconformist call for complete freedom for worship. But changes appeared in another direction which were not so encouraging. Railway communications were fast expanding. The motor-car was beginning to appear. There was the cinema, gramophone and then later the radio. These had an irresistible fascination. Excursions out into the country, holidays, visits to the cinema, the ownership of some vehicle or machine – these were all the order of the day and soon were to become increasingly popular as the years went by. What some people felt alarming was that these changes did not only affect a small minority, the aristocrats or the wealthy middle-class, who had always had the opportunities to enjoy themselves, but a vast number of people, namely, the working classes who had never had the chance for leisure. Materially, politically, and socially the masses were on the march as the shackles of oppression had at last been thrown off. They had gained for themselves more leisure-time by the mere fact that hours in factories and mines had been greatly reduced.

In the wake of the changes in leisure the churches frequently expressed their fears through a moral denunciation of newly found pleasures. Few of the means of communication could be condemned as immoral in themselves. What the churches objected to was that they encouraged a mental attitude in which pleasure assumed a prominent place. People were accused of seeking a leisured life rather than one dominated by work. But as in previous eras there was more than a moral denunciation. Church leaders were aware of the fact that new ways of using leisure were a direct threat to the very existence of the churches. People forsook attendance at public worship for days at the seaside, for rides in motor-cars, for sessions with the gramophone. Sermons, articles in church magazines, and books thumped away at these new forms of activity because of their direct impact on church attendance. But events took their course despite the declamations of Church leaders. Church-going in relative terms declined around the turn of the last century and continued to decline until the 1930s. In all this one is reminded of the basic fear that has always been at the back of the minds of Church leaders that the enemy of religion is a pleasure-seeking society. J. N. Figgis, that extraordinary and prophetic writer of the Edwardian period, held that it was not poverty that kept people away from the churches as so many supposed, among them Horace Mann in his report on the Religious Census of 1851.[3] Rather, it was the growing affluence that was the real enemy of religion – an affluence which was affecting a numerically large section of society. In his *Religion and English Society*, published in 1911, Figgis said that people were using wealth, inherited or earned, for the sake of pleasure and without any reference to religion or morality, except such as forbade baser pleasures.[4] What was happening applied to all classes. He wrote:

> . . . paganisation . . . is due to the great part played in modern life by delocalised irresponsible wealth. This has organised for itself a world of interests which occupies every energy without reference to anything beyond.[5]

And again:

> With the increase of riches and the Americanisation of society (by this I mean a world living apart from the sources of the money which the owners have nothing to do but to spend) there has come waywardness and an indiscipline and all restraints are resented.[6]

Figgis held that when the general atmosphere of society is oriented towards pleasure, religion is faced with a particularly difficult task. It may be unable to make any impact upon society, or else it may lose its essential features due to the permeation of the churches by the pleasure mentality. For Figgis the essential features included the notes of discipline and protest, and these he saw were beginning to disappear in the religion of his day. He believed that the churches would become minority groups and so form religious remnants in society.

To assume that the decline of institutional religion over the past century or so has been due to the rise of leisure-time activities, as some church leaders have prophesied or stated as fact, constitutes too simple an explanation of what has happened to the fortunes of the churches. None the less, an analysis of the growth of leisure-time pursuits during this period is of considerable help in understanding the changes that occurred in the churches at the time and of the attitude of people towards them. In using this model for explanation it would be of value to know how people view religion today and how far they see it as in some ways comparable with a leisure-time pursuit. Should they perceive it in such a light, it seems legitimate to infer that the model put forward is important. More-

over, in looking again at the churches in the nineteenth century,
is it not possible to see that in dealing with rise of leisure, leaders
in some way changed the ethos of the churches in accommodating
them to it?

IV

During research undertaken by the author between 1953 and 1958
in two industrial towns in the northern part of England, some evidence came to light which has bearing on the issue under discussion.[7]
A sample of church members was asked questions which were designed to show their general attitude towards religion. The research
also made use of relevant historical evidence from the local churches.

General attitudes are by no means easy to pin down. In the
attempt to see how church members viewed religion, assumptions
had to be made and simple direct questions asked. One rather crude
way of looking at the problem is to see how much membership of
a church 'costs' individuals. It might be assumed that the more
religion 'costs' the less it can be viewed as a leisure-time pursuit.[8] If
the 'cost' is persecution or death, the practice of religion is hardly
equivalent to membership of a gardening club! If on the other hand
the 'cost' is minimal, religion may be assumed to be lightly esteemed.

Cost to most people is reckoned in terms of money. The churches
usually finance themselves through collections, and money is
required for the upkeep of the church, for the salary of the priest
or minister, for charitable causes, and so on. In the towns surveyed,
Rawmarsh in Yorkshire, and Scunthorpe in Lincolnshire, it was
found that in the mid-1950s people of all ages gave in collections on
average 1*s*. 0*d*. each time they went to church, or if adults only were
taken into consideration, about 1*s*. 6*d*. per attendance. The average
was higher by a few pence in Scunthorpe – the more prosperous
of the towns – and it was slightly higher by the same amount among
Roman Catholics in both towns. It was also greater on average among
members of sects; among certain groups, such as the Pentecostalists,
it was very much above the average. Judged by collections alone it
cannot be said that church members as a whole suffer any severe
pinching of the shoe in maintaining their churches and clergy, or in
contributing to outside causes. Admittedly, many church people give
in other ways, for example, through bazaars, house collections or
covenants. A number of the church members interviewed said they

gave quite a lot in such ways but by and large most confessed that what they put in the church plate was a shilling or two. Yet some of the respondents also admitted that they or their husbands earned £10, £15, £20 a week.

In attempting to see how church members view their religion, and at the same time not being forgetful of the assumptions that have been made about 'cost', the following question was asked of church members:

> Do you find in the practice of your religion, in what you are asked to believe or do, anything that can be said to be unpleasant? You do it because you are asked to do it, the church tells you you ought to do it. Even Christ told his followers that they had to suffer for his sake. Is there anything you give up for the sake of being a church member?

The answers to this question revealed not the demands of religion or the suffering involved, but the pleasure that religion gave to those who followed it. For many the practice of religion meant going to church and that respondents thoroughly liked. Some of the comments that were given in response to the question are stated below:

> You get lightened and lifted up at the service – you've nothing to lose.

> No, if there was anything unpleasant I wouldn't go.

> You're not forced to do anything you don't want to. If we work for church we all do it voluntary.

> I enjoy going to church.

> I would not do it if I did not want to do it.

> I enjoy every minute of it. I go and scrub: wash windows and wash pots.

> It doesn't cost me anything – there's nothing unpleasant or difficult about it.

> I do most things I want to as long as I am not hurting anyone.

> It costs nothing – the church is the cheapest entertainment in the world. You visit an (old) church, you get a grand sight, and you just put a few pence in't box.

But not all the answers were in this vein. About 30% of the sample of 135 who were questioned admitted that there were aspects of religion they felt distasteful but which had to be accepted. When respondents were asked to be more specific about what they meant, the answers proved to be so vague that careful classification was impossible. Some of the more coherent answers were in terms of 'cost' and these are given below according to denominational grouping. The most outspoken came from members of the sects. Some of their members said: 'Folk gossip a bit.' 'People snub me.'

'You get called all sorts.' 'M'husband objects to m' going.' Other sectarians commented:

> I get a blessing every time I go. I kind of get lighthearted. Christ suffered ridicule. Odd times I would like to go dancing but I don't. Father tends to ridicule me about it in company – shows me up at times.

> You get your leg pulled because you don't go drinking.

> You've got to forgive those you have been done hardest by.

> The Christian life is costly. You've got to forsake the world. You're in the world but not of it.

Roman Catholics offered one or two direct comments:

> It's hard to be a Catholic. I say, Am I doing wrong? If I am, I have to confess it. There's no hypocrisy here.

> It's not more difficult than any other, though it is sometimes difficult to make your confession. (Lapsed).

> The Catholic religion is a harder religion. You have to get up early, for example, for the 7.30 mass. More effort is required.

Among Free Church people points of hardship were less visible. Some of them were:

> I get criticized for being a Christian. I don't swear – they have a skit at you.

> Others go to public houses: they think I am not right because I don't go.

> Sometimes in looking after people you're not fond of.

> If the lady died next door – she's difficult to get on with – I would have to go round and sympathize with her relatives.

> My husband disapproves of religion.

> You have to give up the bright social set.

> The standard of some lay preaching puts you off the service.

Anglicans were the least sure about the question:

> Sometimes they skit at you at work.

> Yes, if you go to church as we go, you're all the time paying out.

> Getting up in the morning for Holy Communion.

> It's more than an ordinary irritation to come face to face with the same sins week by week. (Schoolboy, 18 years old.)

The immediate conclusion from these, and other comments not given, is that if any people suffer hardship for religious reasons, even the mildest form of public hostility, it is those who are members of the sects, particularly members who are Pentecostalists, Jehovah's Witnesses, and to a lesser extent members of the Salvation Army. From what they said there is little reason to doubt that at work, in evangelical labours, and in their personal lives, many are snubbed by their fellows, or ridiculed in the local community, or despised by their own kith and kin. Most though not quite all the respondents who referred to hardships at work by reason of the comments or actions of their mates were associated with the sects. People who were members of the churches were generally accepted, though the occasional Free Churchman found himself disliked over his attitude towards total abstinence. In considering another form of 'cost' Roman Catholics mentioned having to go to Mass each Sunday, sometimes early in the morning; and what was more common was reference to the unpleasantness of having to go to confession. By and large members of the Church of England and the Nonconformist churches were hard pressed to be as concrete as this. The very occasional and pious Anglican would mention rising for an 8 a.m. service of Holy Communion. There was very little awareness among Anglicans and Free Churchmen of anything bordering on sacrifice or on the unpleasant. It was also observed in the same survey – and there is some parallel here – that Anglicans and Free Churchmen were the least specific when they were asked to give examples of sin.

This empirical evidence, to be sure very limited, at least suggests from the lips of church members themselves that the practice of religion today makes few stringent demands. There is the need of further surveys along this line; and also inquiries from people who have left the churches, perhaps through difficulties not acknowledged by those who persist in their membership of the churches. But from what has just been stated, it is clear that the practice of religion involves little that can be called unpleasant or distasteful. The demands that it makes are probably less exacting than those associated with the carrying out of an occupation or those which come with marriage and family life. Attending church appears to be akin to going to the cinema or the theatre, or attending evening classes, or again visiting one's friends. The pursuits are recreational. If they do not fulfil this function, they are dropped and membership ceases. Church people admitted that if they did not enjoy the services they would not go. If they derived no pleasure from the hymns or from the sermon they would stay away. In their minds' eye they pictured the local church as some form of spiritual 'home' which gave them pleasures corresponding to those they received by being in their own home.

It is undeniable that contemporary institutional religion possesses certain social qualities which in the minds of many people allow it to be seen as some form of leisure-time pursuit. The qualities that have emerged, it might be argued, have been brought about by the growth of secularization. Intertwined with this growth there has been an accompanying evaluation of religion which has given it a relatively unimportant place in the affairs of men. For example, the state no longer dogmatizes in the matter of church allegiance. There is freedom to worship in any denomination and freedom not to worship at all. The state refuses to be involved in theological niceties and thereby declares to the world their relative unimportance. For that reason, if for no other, religious persecution is looked upon as being in the last analysis irrelevant, if not inhuman. Along with secularization there has grown a scientific culture and at the same time there has been the development of mass leisure-time activities. However, the fact that people consciously or unconsciously hold religion to be a leisure-time pursuit can be attributed not only to forces which might be said to be operative around the churches or even against them, but to those that appeared within them. The churches themselves, howbeit unwittingly, have encouraged people to view religion in such a manner as to suggest that it is in some measure at least a leisure-time pursuit.

V

During the nineteenth century many of the churches, especially the Nonconformist churches, underwent changes in their ethos which were in a direction away from what might be termed strictly religious activities. A study of such changes in the Methodist churches – and it was such churches which were of considerable importance among the lower middle classes and to a lesser degree among the working classes – is rewarding. To look through Methodist circuit plans and old newspapers for the early part of the nineteenth century is to be confronted with the fact that nearly every Methodist meeting was to the outward eye solidly 'religious'. Notes of sobriety and seriousness ring through the description of a special service, or the holding of a prayer-meeting, or the taking of a class. The only possible time of limited relaxation was to be found in the love-feast, and around the middle of the century that institution was to disappear. By the 1870s a new pattern had emerged. For one thing less attention was focused on the prayer-meeting, the class meeting, the open-air meeting, and more was paid to week-day activities in which there were elements bordering on entertainment, light relaxation or general education. About this time also Sunday school anniversaries come into prominence and the annual jubilations extend from Sunday to week-day. Eye-witnesses speak of the splendour of the services, the excellency of the choir, the virtue of the soloist, the oratory of the preacher, and the brilliance of the lecturer.

Most of these qualities were either unknown or were unheeded in the early days of Methodism. The early worship services of the Methodists were characterized by their congregational participation, by enthusiastic and noisy singing, and by a fairly 'free' form of service. A century or so later trained choirs, anthems, solos, and a rigid pattern of worship calling for little spontaneity on the part of the congregation were the order of the day. The quality of musical production was a high priority in the larger Methodist chapels, Wesleyan or Primitive. Worshippers found themselves listeners and spectators who were acted upon as passive receivers and this was particularly the case where the emphasis was placed on the sermon which the listener keenly anticipated. The architecture of the larger Methodist chapels which were built in the latter half of the nineteenth century encouraged the concert atmosphere with the choir facing the people and the minister being situated in the centre of the 'stage'. Indeed, the layout of the larger Nonconformist chapels in the second half of the nineteenth century closely resembled that of the secular concert halls and the provincial town halls which were then being built.

The Church of England did not undergo the same kinds of changes that were so noticeable in the Methodist and other Nonconformist churches. For one thing, the Church of England was bound by the Prayer Book which called for a set form of service. For another, its established position gave it a sense of authority which asked for obedience on the part of its followers. The Church maintained a conformity to a tradition rather than a striving for popularity among the masses. The Anglican Church was of course greatly influenced by the Evangelical and High Church revivals but these tended to move in the direction of traditionalism and towards an

ethos of some bygone age – to the early Church, to the Church of
the Caroline divines, or, in the case of the Anglo-Catholics, to the
Church of the Middle Ages. None the less, innovations where they
were in keeping with the spirit of the Prayer Book were introduced
and were frequently copied from the successful tactics of the Nonconformists. Evening services were begun in the mid-nineteenth
century to prevent servants being tempted to attend chapel services.
Hymns, so popular among the Methodists, were given considerable
place in Morning and Evening Prayer.

Where the Established Church tried to adapt itself to meet the
people was in encouraging socio-religious activities which were very
much part of the ethos of the Nonconformist churches in the latter
half of the nineteenth century. The term socio-religious is taken to
mean an activity associated with a church which contains elements
which are not strictly religious in the conventional meaning of the
word. Organizations in the Church of England such as the Mothers'
Union, men's fellowships and youth clubs come within the category.
Such organizations usually had at at some stage of their meetings a
short service, a prayer, a Bible reading, but other activities could
vary from playing games (innocent ones, of course) to sewing, and
from collecting clothes for the poor to listening to lectures. From a
virtual non-existence at the beginning of the nineteenth century,
these groups had gathered great momentum by its closing decades.
Nonconformists were prominent not least in attempting the informal
education of their members, who were frequently drawn from the
underprivileged sections of society. Anniversaries were accompanied
by lectures with such titles as: 'A Peep in my Album – or Portraits
of real life' (1868); 'Health' (1891); 'Steps to Fortune, rung by rung,
or a Purpose in Life' (1900); 'Love, Courtship and Marriage –
humorous rather than serious' (1902).[9] There were literary societies
connected with some Nonconformist churches, and the Wesleyan
Methodists introduced what they called a Mutual Improvement
Society for social and religious purposes which included musical
items, stories and talks. The Band of Hope claimed to give better
entertainment than could be had in the public houses. The Pleasant
Sunday Afternoon classes, strongly sponsored by the Primitive
Methodists, attempted to draw working-class men (and later women)
by offering entertainment mingled with religion. The meetings were
described as 'brief, bright and brotherly'. At the turn of the century
one Methodist chapel which had a membership of 100 found as many

as 600 people attracted to the Sunday PSA meeting. Shortly after the First World War the PSA with its emphasis on entertainment disappeared. However, socio-religious groups as a whole persisted and in particular they tended to be focused on the young. The socio-religious activities remain part of the contemporary ethos of nearly all churches today except perhaps certain sectarian groups. The Roman Catholic Church was slow in accepting them and it is probably true to say that the socio-religious groups in that church were peripheral in the late nineteenth century compared to their place in other churches. The Church of England was always slightly behind the Nonconformist churches in encouraging such activities. The clergy of the Establishment with their middle-class background perceived entertainment and relaxation as private affairs to be enjoyed in the seclusion of a comfortable home. Nonconformist ministers, especially certain Methodists, saw that recreation for the working classes had to be organized outside the cramped and often squalid homes of the poor. Hence Good Friday Teas; Christmas Day concerts; and PSAs. These were unheard of activities in the churches of the Establishment in provincial towns. Anglican churches were, and still are, often viewed as being cold by Nonconformist standards just because there existed in the Nonconformist churches an ethos which tended to be open and associated with enjoyment and pleasure. However, such was the success of Nonconformity in the middle of the nineteenth century, and so obvious was it that it was meeting the 'needs of the people' that Anglicans adopted similar methods though, as it had already been said, they did so in connection with socio-religious activities rather than with the services of the church.

It is not too much to suggest that in the period of say 1870–1914, the chapels, certainly in the large towns, performed the function of providing entertainment for local people.[10] One might be so bold to say that in some respects the chapels were the forerunners of the provincial theatres and cinemas. Certainly the local chapels attempted to perform as many functions as possible for the community and that of entertainment was by no means overlooked.

Why was it that the Nonconformist churches, and to some extent the Established Church, moved in the direction they did in championing socio-religious activities and in retailoring their services? There were at least two reasons for making such changes. First there was a moral, perhaps theological, issue. Certain sections of society were seeking education, even entertainment. People with a newly acquired status, with more time for leisure, as well as those still suffering from poverty and from evil social conditions, wanted help, encouragement, and leadership. The advantages enjoyed by the middle classes ought to be extended, it was felt, to those who heretofore had never experienced them. The churches were of the opinion that they had a mission to meet the 'need' and to act as agents for education, leadership, and entertainment. And second, the churches realized they were not graced with the active allegiance of the entire population. The 1851 Religious Census[11] confirmed what many observers had thought, namely, that large numbers of people were not actively associated with the churches. Leaders were only too conscious of the failure to stem the forces of secularization, and the consequence was that they adopted any means they could legitimately employ to attract outsiders to the church. Socio-religious activities in which the religious pill was covered with a coating of social sugar became one obvious method. It was thought that such activities would be useful in preventing members from sliding away from the church, as well as attracting those who had little interest in it.[12] But the venture had unhappy consequences. When more attractive forms of entertainment appeared – the cinema, the radio, the car – the force of the more attractive won the day. If entertainment and recreation are the points of issue then people go where their inclinations lead them. That Methodist chapels in some cases became cinemas and public libraries in the 1930s was more than a coincidence. It was part of a foreseeable social process. The introduction of socio-religious activities and the efforts made by church leaders to attract people to the churches by offering them social facilities and entertainment thus appears to have created in people's minds the notion that church affiliation is in part associated with a leisure-time pursuit. The churches themselves were instrumental in bringing about such an outlook. Secular leisure-time pursuits became a rival to religion as religion set itself up as a rival to leisure-time pursuits. The truth of the matter is that if A is thought to be a rival of B, the entities A and B can be legitimately compared.

VI

To say that contemporary religion is of the form of a leisure-time pursuit is not to suggest that every act or belief can be viewed as being of that order. Such a position would be absurd. Deeply religious people (and there were such in the two towns studied) would probably be prepared to suffer hardship, even persecution for their faith. They would be the last to suggest that their religion was akin to a leisure-pastime. Also, those facing grief and bereavement, those suffering from severe illness and finding help in religion, those trying to lead moral lives in the face of temptation, are hardly likely to view religion as something which can be compared to an institution for recreation or relaxation. No one would be so foolish as to suggest that membership of a church is in some way equivalent to membership of say, a hiking club or a political party. Nor can the decline of religion be adequately explained by reference to no other factor than the growth of leisure-time activities in recent decades. Religion is much too complex a phenomenon to be dealt with so simply.

What this paper has attempted to do has been to raise for consideration the notion that modern institutional religion contains social characteristics which have strong parallels with some of the essential social qualities of leisure-time pursuits. It has been impossible to do little more than offer rather limited and disjointed evidence from historical and survey sources. But what has been presented is sufficient to justify at least the possibility of seeing that contemporary religion in the eyes of many people is a leisure-time activity, which to a very large extent is the outcome of the churches finding themselves to be one of a very large number of voluntary organizations. If the model that has been put forward is useful then it deserves further application in the examination of the changes that have occurred in the religious institutions of western society in recent years.

NOTES

1. B. R. Wilson, *Religion in Secular Society*, London: Watts, 1966, p. 198.

2. I. Craven, article on 'Leisure' in the *Encyclopedia of the Social Sciences*, New York: Macmillan, 1935.

3. See W. S. F. Pickering, 'The 1851 Religious Census – A Useless Experiment?', *British Journal of Sociology* 18, 1967, pp. 382–407.

4. *Religion and English Society*, London: Longmans, 1911, p. 28.

5. *Op. cit.*, p. 26.

6. *Op. cit.*, p. 31.

7. See W. S. F. Pickering, *The Place of Religion in the Social Structure of two Industrial Towns, Rawmarsh (Yorkshire) and Scunthorpe (Lincolnshire)*, unpub-

lished Ph.D. thesis, London University, 1958, Chapter IX. Some of the material in that chapter is used in this paper.

8. It must be admitted that certain hobbies and pursuits, such as photography and keeping horses, are costly in terms of money but the overall effect is said to be pleasurable and worth the cost.

9. All these examples are from records relating to Rawmarsh and Scunthorpe.

10. This was openly acknowledged and was often a point of concern amongst some Methodist lay people in the two towns studied.

11. See W. S. F. Pickering, *op. cit.*

12. Another factor ought not to be overlooked. It was that the Nonconformist churches had at last become accepted and they wished to show to society that their members too were 'cultured' and able to enjoy and organize what the aristocracy and older middle classes had held dear to them. The Nonconformists wanted to demonstrate this within their churches. Some observers might be tempted to see this movement as the change in status of Nonconformist bodies from 'sect' to 'church'. But to use such concepts raises too many issues to be dealt with in this paper.

5 Towards an Analysis of Contemporary Cults

John Jackson and *Ray Jobling*

MUCH of the literature of the sociology of religion concerns itself with aspects of the typology of religious groups initially developed by Ernst Troeltsch, following a distinction drawn by Max Weber, and usually loosely referred to as the 'Church/Sect Typology'.[1] Troeltsch regarded his typology as a taxonomic device for the purpose of contrasting different *Christian* religious groups, and more especially the illumination of differences in social organization between the typical Christian 'sect' and 'church'. While there have been attempts to adjust the typology for the analysis of non-Christian religions, subsequent sociological study has concentrated on the analysis of the characteristics, structure and dynamics of the Christian sect type. In recent years valuable insights have been derived from the isolation of sub-types of the sect and from the consideration of the posited development of sects into denominations. The notion of the established sect which does not take on a pure denominational form has been a further sophistication. Detailed study of the denomination has received more limited attention, and while churches have, of course, been the subject of analysis there have been few attempts to consider them in the context of the more general typology.

One type of religious and organizational form not usually associated with Troeltsch's original formulation is the cult. It does, however, occupy a not inconsiderable place in the literature of the field and is frequently employed as an additional type. However, there is a diversity and discrepancy of usage which is difficult to account for, especially since most analysts pay lip-service at least to the influence of Howard Becker's treatment of 'cult' in his *Systematic Sociology*.[2] Possibly one of the central problems has been that the concept and term already have meanings and an established usage within the fields of anthropology and theology, as well as a somewhat pejorative connotation in lay usage.

There are two distinct anthropological meanings. The cult may be seen as 'the totality of the religious institutions of a society, particularly pre-literate societies'.[3] More often the anthropologist will adopt a more limited definition whereby the cult becomes 'a body of religious beliefs and practices associated with a particular god or set of gods constituting a specialised part of the religious institutions of a society. By inclusion the officiants and practitioners in such a part of the religious structure of a society are sometimes called a cult.'[4] It is rare for a sociologist to adopt either of these anthropological formulations. However, the second approach may be combined with a quasi-theological definition. T. F. O'Dea, for example, suggests that 'that complex of gesture, word, and symbolic vehicle which is the central religious phenomenon we call the cult, is first of all an acting of feelings, attitudes, and relationships'.[5] O'Dea is here speaking of relationships with sacred objects, and the acts are purely expressive, having no instrumental value in themselves. Thus the cult becomes the sum total of 'speech, gesture, song, sacramental meals, and sacrifice associated with sacred objects'.[6] The Marian cult of Roman Catholicism would therefore be the body of beliefs and rites specifically associated by believers with the Virgin.

Sociologists usually avoid popular or dictionary definitions which are too imprecise, ambiguous, or evaluative for their purposes. At least one writer on cults (admittedly not a professional sociologist) has, however, followed a general dictionary and incorporated in his definition the assumption of adverse evaluation of certain religious groups, describing the cult as 'a religion regarded as unorthodox or spurious, also a minority religious group holding beliefs so regarded'.[7]

However Becker, whose discussion has provided the basis for most sociological conceptualization, suggests that the term cult be applied where tendencies toward religion of a 'strictly private, personal character . . . come to full fruition'. The cult is a 'very amorphous, loose-textured, uncondensed type of social structure.'[8] The goal of the adherent is that of purely personal ecstatic experience, salvation, comfort, and mental or physical healing; whereas the church member or sect follower has a definite commitment to the maintenance of the structure itself – the continuation of the corporate body of committed believers. One does not join a cult, one simply chooses to believe particular theories or follow certain practices. No one, Becker maintains, need give consent to the decision. In this respect the cult differs from the sect, where consent and recognition of fellowship by the other followers is of central importance. Further, the experience of fellowship would not provide the typical cult adherent with a sense of satisfaction or well-being. His or her sources of emotional satisfaction are purely personal and internal.

David Martin, in a discussion owing more to Ernst Troeltsch than most writers on cults, has asserted that the fundamental criterion for determining the cult type is ideological and structural individualism.[9] Since he regards the 'fellowship principle' as an essential of Christianity, Martin relegates cults to a sub-Christian status and discusses them in the context of the dechristianization of belief. The ephemeral character of cults is partially explained by this lack of a sense of fellowship which Martin views as necessary for historical continuity. Benton Johnson has lent support to Martin's position on the non-Christian nature of cults.[10] He maintains that whereas Christian groups reflect the 'cosmic image' of emissary prophecy, where specific demands are made in terms of the followers' behaviour and social relationships, the cult's outlook is a matter of a reflection of exemplary prophecy, which provides for lack of concern with mundane affairs and concentration on perfection in personal spiritual exercises. Johnson is here breaking away from the more conventional typology in favour of Max Weber's treatment of types of prophet and prophecy.

Johnson and Martin fail to do justice to the full potentiality of Troeltsch's original contribution.[11] Troeltsch is in fact analysing not cults as such, but 'mysticism'. He suggests that one of the sociological peculiarities of this form of spiritual religion is indeed individualism, but it is not of a kind separating individuals from the world by a conscious hostility to social relationships and worldliness. Nor is fellowship with other believers rejected as such. Fellowship among mystics is not enforced by separateness and a greater ethical severity than that imposed in the wider society, as is the case with the sect. Mysticism relies on spiritual fellowship, rather than the establishment of formal organizations and societies. Where mystics do form groups there is no intention that they shall be exclusive, taking the place of the churches as the typical emergent sect would do. The groups are 'intimate circles for edification' which are flexible, constantly forming and re-forming as the spiritual needs of the participants demand. Their religion is spiritual, super-ecclesiastical, syncretistic, indifferent, unfanatical. Unlike Martin and Johnson, Troeltsch recognizes this form of religion as a constant, if at times weak, theme in the Christian tradition.

Bryan Wilson has rejected the concept of cult, preferring to treat the beliefs, practices, and groups considered elsewhere as cults as a sub-type of the sect.[12] Initially Wilson subsumed these under the heading of the 'Gnostic sect' which offers a special esoteric teaching. Conventional Christian eschatology is replaced by a greater optimism and the complex of mystical doctrines seeks to replace secular, scientific explanations offering an alternative cosmology, anthropology, psychology. The utility of the gnosis in everyday life is stressed and success, self-realization, health, wealth and happiness are all promised. Leaders style themselves as teachers or guides. Other churches and belief systems are treated with indifference or an attitude of superiority. Martin has criticized Wilson for treating as Christian sects groups lacking the Christian fellowship principle and frequently 'assimilated to secular goals'.[13] For Martin, the sect typically involves a 'degree of radical rejection of society which the etymology (of the term sect) implies'.[14] Wilson himself has more recently restyled his Gnostic sub-type as 'Manipulationist sect' in which he stresses the innovatory character of the movements and, following a contribution by Martin Marty, applies the designation *positively oriented*.[15] In this way he makes clear his rejection of Martin's views that sects are always negatively oriented, i.e. hostile to the world.

These several discussions display ambivalence and ambiguity in conceptualization and analytical application. It is possible, however, to draw them together. We prefer to distinguish between two social forms under the general heading of 'cult'. First, there is the mystic-religious cult where certain esoteric practices are pursued in order to maximize the votary's individual experience. This experience is defined by the cult votary himself in religious terms and the orientation is primarily religious. The wider society is most frequently conceived of as an irrelevancy, and opposition to the world only occurs where the spiritual religious life of the individual is impinged upon. The second form of cult is in contrast world-affirming and esoteric practices are here adopted as manipulative techniques which will be instrumental in enhancing the success, prestige, and power of the votary in the world. In orientation such movements are primarily non-religious, though quasi-religious practices figure among their

D

techniques. We shall therefore style this form the quasi-religious cult.

The distinction between the two forms is analytical and should be treated as dynamic. In so far as they can constantly define and re-define the situation in new ways, giving new meaning to their practices, cult votaries may themselves be at one time mystic-religious and at another quasi-religious in terms of motivation and orientation to the world. It is possible for a movement to be initiated for the purpose of exploiting particular needs or fears of a section of the population, appealing perhaps to a desire for physical or mental healing. Many of those attracted may, however, be religious seekers with little or no concern for the secular-instrumental value of the cult practices, but rather concerned with their value in enhancing spiritual, religious awareness. The two kinds of votary may at one and the same time participate in the same movement. It may be that both secular and religious motivations are involved in the case of a particular individual. But this may be so with involvement in the Church, denomination or sect. A pilgrimage to Lourdes is at once an expression of religious devotion and faith and also a matter of the secular hope for healing. Movements may begin as quasi-religious, developing over time into the mystic-religious form – the reverse being equally possible. In the case of Dianetics-Scientology, the original secular scientific character has been eroded and references to the Church of Scientology are now common. Both forms of cult, we would suggest, are non-exclusive, making no restriction on the votary's attachment to specific groups or subscription to other belief systems. Typically both forms of cult are tolerant of other belief systems – including science – though they frequently believe these to be inferior. Both are also individualistic in the sense suggested by Troeltsch and formal organizations, while existing, make no cere-monial or ritual demands on votaries. Nor is collective affirmation of belief or direct 'face to face' social contact required. In these respects cults differ markedly from sects.

Most writers have connected cult individualism, syncretism, and their frequent secular-instrumentalism with the social condition of modern city life, i.e. have treated these as expected features of the *gesellschaft*. Our mystic-religious cults occur as easily in a non-urbanized structural setting, and we would suggest that cultural factors may play a role in the emergence and development of such cults, for example in the Orient. It is certainly true that cults in their quasi-religious form flourish in urban conditions. W. E. Mann has shown that even in a predominantly rural environment quasi-religious cult votaries were drawn from a rapidly growing city rather than the countryside.[16] Mann seeks to establish, as the cult-generating structural condition *par excellence*, extreme urbanism, where the established social supports of a 'balanced' community are lacking. One would therefore expect cults to flourish, as they have, in the rapidly expanding cities of the American and Canadian West in the nineteenth and twentieth centuries. The social groups most prone to cult involvement are, for Mann, the middle-aged, middle-class, frequently single and female inhabitants of rapidly urbanizing and suburbanizing areas.

This whole discussion could be set in the context of the long tradition of the analysis of social disorganization, and anomie, as a condition of certain types of social structure conducive to the emergence of deviant or nonconformist perspectives. In terms of Robert Merton's typology of modes of adaptation to anomie our quasi-religious cults would best be described as 'innovatory'.[17] They basically accept societal goals but introduce and positively sanction novel means for their achievement. The mystic-religious cults would be 'retreatist' in that they find the cultural goals irrelevant and ignore generally accepted institutionalized forms of behaviour. It could be argued that they are closest to the form of adaptation styled by Merton as 'rebellion' in so far as they presumably would prefer a greatly modified social and cultural structure. Cult votaries, however, seek a new way of life for themselves alone and then only on a spiritual plane. In certain instances this can lead to violent behaviour, though characteristically it is violence against the self, for example suicide in an attempt to remove oneself permanently to a separate spiritual existence beyond the threshold of death.

We reject the view that cults attract individuals with pathological personality structures, on the grounds that there is no empirical evidence in support of it. None the less, it is a view held by a number of influential analysts, including Neil Smelser who has referred to cult votaries as possessing semi-paranoid personality characteristics derived from distinctive familial experiences (e.g. a rejecting father) and strains stemming from childhood experiences.

There is some evidence that cults may develop into sects and that conversely sectarians may over time, or in the second generation, begin to view their beliefs and practices in a secular-instrumental way, or alternatively individualize, spiritualize and mysticize their religion in a fashion typical of the cult votary. These processes may be observed in the cases of Christian Science and Quakerism. The former began as part of the general New Thought cult movement, over time sectarian characteristics were displayed and eventually sect-establishment occurred. Some of the second generation, however, have reverted to the motivational and organizational forms typical of the cult. Quakerism beginning as a radical sect has undergone denominationalization, and there may even be a churchward movement. It is, however, possible to contend that Quakerism has for some become a cult.[19] Scientology, initially a self-consciously secular cult, has taken on a mystic-religious character (and there are a number of schismatic groups which have been more clearly religious in orientation), and recent developments would imply a sectward movement.[20]

It would be unwise, however, to suggest that the sect is merely the institutionalized cult – either of the mystic-religious type or the quasi-religious type. The tendencies observed in some cults towards organizational and institutional consolidation may be derived from necessity – a reaction to opposition which places the cult in the same 'opposed' position to society as that which has characterized the experience of the sect. This can be observed in recent publications of 'Scientology' which deals with the subject of 'Critics of Scientology'. This movement has been for some years exposed to unfavourable publicity which culminated in an investigation by a Commission of Enquiry of the State of Victoria in Australia during 1965.[21] Now on the defensive the cult adopts attitudes which are aimed at condemning the detractors while reassuring 'the faithful'. One quotation from a 1967 publication will suffice to illustrate the point:

'Now get this as a technical *fact*, not a hopeful idea. Every time we have investigated the background of a critic of Scientology we have found *crimes* for which that person or group could be imprisoned under existing law. We do *not* find critics of Scientology who do not have criminal pasts. Over and over we prove this.[22]

Clearly there is a fairly strong negative orientation present here which supports the sectward movement already referred to resulting from external opposition to the beliefs or practices of the cult votaries. In such a situation one also finds a hostile orientation developing toward other belief systems and science, and a greater emphasis being placed on aspects of 'fellowship' which will retain the support of the followers.

The distinctive qualities of the cult – those qualities which might set the votaries apart from less fortunate 'outsiders' – may also come to assume transcendental features. The cult leader may cease being merely a technician purveying the instrumental benefits that are offered and become a figure possessed of charismatic qualities which set him and by implication his teaching on a pedestal of authority. One may also see in the development of a cult the creation of those conditions of 'fellowship' noted by Becker and Martin as characteristic of the sect. Indeed 'fellowship' may be a necessary consequence of the defensive postures which have been assumed by such movements as Scientology in response to attack. It is notable that recent literature sent out by the movement has stressed the social benefits to be derived from participation in courses at Saint Hill Manor and suggests that there is a move away from instrumental individual therapy toward group therapy as part of Scientology. There is also, and this directly reflects the anxiety caused by attacks aimed at the 'illegitimate' practice of healing by the movement, a move away from therapy itself. No longer does the movement claim therapeutic capacity as such but offers training to its adherents.

Scientology appears to be increasing those elements in its structure which Becker has suggested are most appropriate to the sect. It offers not just a body of beliefs which individuals are free to take or leave alone as they choose. Increasingly it offers a structured way of life, a community within a community, in which the highest fellowship is to be found with other devotees and not outside the movement. Encouragement for this tendency is provided by promotion techniques designed to encourage group solidarity. The list of 'Clears' as a kind of Roll of Honour is now matched in the literature of the movement by birth, marriage and death announcements and 'social notes' which can help to keep the faithful in touch. Even the emphasis still given to the initials A.D. to describe the number of years 'After Dianetics' suggests the extension of the alternative belief system into a more comprehensive focus than the cultic.[23]

We do not want to carry this illustration too far, however, nor make too much of the symbolic aspects of 'culture' formation within a particular organization. What is apparent is that as cults of this kind develop they are liable to accommodate to the social needs of their members. This serves to alter the particularistic and instrumental relationship of the members into one of more universal significance embodying a sense of community and shared experience and participation – in the cultic practices and experience – and also, in an increasingly important sense in the corporate life.

The illustrations drawn from Scientology that we have used can be matched from a number of other contemporary cults that are active in Britain. Moral Rearmament, for instance, has, even from its early days at Oxford, emphasized the group and fellowship aspects as well as stressing a broader goal as the result of individual commitment. This movement again incorporates elements of participation which depend upon other group members to some extent. This characteristic is apparent in more obviously 'take it or leave it' cult such as those concerned with psychical phenomena or UFO's.

In discussing these tendencies in the cult we have argued against a rigid distinction between sect and cult. In doing so we have been concerned to try to distinguish those different elements of belief systems which are found in both religious and other social movements. In general, most cults appear to be of either the *mystic religious* or the *quasi-religious* type, but this distinction embodies the capacity within each of these types to embrace the purely instrumental and particularist gratification and also non-instrumental (concerned with others, the world, etc.) and finally a transcendental element. The cult in common with other established religious types (church, denomination and sect) thus offers or is likely to develop all three elements to greater or lesser degree in response to the orientation of followers and the development of the belief system in response to organizational pressures.

The typical cult will lie between the highly unstructured decision to believe in the cult suggested by Becker and the definite commitment to the structure by which he characterizes the church or sect member. The orientation is likely to remain individualistic in all the forms the cult may emphasize. It is significant that Moral Rearmament is a movement which claims it can change the world by changing individuals and that individual fulfilment of the instrumental requirements – abstinence, treatment, process or whatever – is a prior condition for participation in the organizational structure. Once the individual has made his commitment to the cult he cannot escape the implicit commitment of fellowship – with other flat-earthers, fire-worshippers or spiritualists – should they happen to meet or should circumstances develop the social consequences of their belief.

Movement from an essentially instrumental quasi-religious cult to one in which transcendental elements are well-developed can be seen in the case of the Aetherius Society.[24] This movement has moved during the course of fourteen years from a largely instrumental phase to one that emphasizes the transcendental elements of the belief system. Thus a quasi-religious cult of flying saucers and space people has developed first in terms of the possibilities of world salvation and finally to the assertion of divine guidance in the fulfilment of transcendental values. The central feature of the transformation was the discovery of the 'Master Jesus' (currently described in their literature as the Avatar Jesus) as one of the members of the Space Parliament. The deliverance of his Twelve New Blessings through the mediumship of the founder George King formed the basis of both collective and individual prayer and worship.

In this paper we have attempted to discuss the cult in the context of the analytical dimensions which have been applied to different belief systems. We do not assume that the cult is a purely secular phenomenon but rather emphasize the presence of elements of cult within all religious bodies as well as the element of collective and transcendent concern which may appear in movements which do not necessarily or initially subscribe to them. By virtue of the fact that the cult offers a possibility of cure or satisfaction, wealth or success, beauty or wisdom, salvation or strength, which cannot be gained through 'the normal channels' it threatens those normal channels and their authority. For some this may be enough to provide the key which unlocks a whole new science, a whole new world, a whole cosmology.

Richard Mathison, in a lively descriptive popular account of cults which is principally concerned to warn readers of the dangers of charlatans, has written that the common bond of all cults is that they answer the call of seekers who are restless and hungry for the flash of insight beyond the mundane world without mystery, a nugget of forgotten love which will bring them quickly to the feet of a true 'godhead'.[25]

The cult must remain to some degree on the fringes of institutional religion but it cannot be classified as being essentially different from religious belief systems. Like the adherents of other religious forms cult votaries are seekers after something, whether perceived only in instrumental terms or not, which may lead them into wider concerns at broader social and transcendental levels than were first apparent. There is no doubt that those so attracted may often fall victim to charlatans and that many cult practitioners may take advantage of their followers' gullibility. This fact, however, does not detract from the general arguments set out above.

NOTES

1. Ernst Troeltsch, *The Social Teaching of the Christian Churches*, Eng. trans., 1931, reprinted New York: Harper Torchbooks, 1960; *From Max Weber: Essays in Sociology* (ed. H. H. Gerth and C. W. Mills), London: Routledge and Kegan Paul, 1948.
2. Howard Becker, *Systematic Sociology*. New York: Wiley and Sons, 1932. Rodney Stark has pointed out that the recent resurgence of scholarly interest in religion has yet to produce a sophisticated analysis of the cult, in 'A Taxonomy of Religious Experience', *Journal for the Scientific Study of Religion* 5, 1965.
3. W. L. Kolb in J. Gould and W. L. Kolb: *A Dictionary of the Social Sciences*, London: Tavistock Publications, 1964, pp. 151 f.
4. *Loc. cit.*
5. T. F. O'Dea, *The Sociology of Religion*, Englewood Clifs: Prentice Hill, 1966.
6. *Ibid.*
7. Anthony A. Hoekema, *The Four Major Cults*, Grand Rapids: Eerdmans, 1963, and Exeter: The Paternoster Press, 1964, p. 374.
8. *Op. cit.*, especially pp. 624–42; quotation from p. 627.
9. David A. Martin: *Pacifism*, London: Routledge and Kegan Paul, 1966.
10. Benton Johnson: 'On Church and Sect', *American Sociological Review* 28, 1963, pp. 539–49.
11. *Op. cit.*
12. Bryan A. Wilson: *Sects and Society*, London: Heinemann, 1961; and 'An Analysis of Sect Development', *American Sociological Review* 24, 1959, pp. 3–15.
13. *Op. cit.*, p. 200.
14. *Ibid.*
15. Bryan R. Wilson: 'Typologie des Sectes dans une Perspective Dynamique et Comparative', *Archives de Sociologie des Religions* 16, July–Dec. 1963, pp. 49–63; and *Religion in Secular Society*, London: Watts, 1966. See also Martin Marty, 'Sects and Cults', *Annals of the American Academy of Political and Social Science*, Vol. 332, November 1966, pp. 125–34.
16. W. E. Mann: *Sect, Cult and Church in Alberta*, Toronto: University of Toronto Press, 1955. The city involved is Calgary, Alberta, Canada.
17. Robert K. Merton: *Social Theory and Social Structure*, New York, 1964.
18. Neil J. Smelser: *A Theory of Collective Behaviour*, London: Routledge and Kegan Paul, 1962.
19. On Christian Science see B. R. Wilson, *Sects and Society*, 1960. On Quakers see Howard Becker, *op. cit.*, and Elizabeth Isichei, 'From Sect to Denomination among English Quakers', *British Journal of Sociology* 15(3), 1964, pp. 207–22.
20. See J. A. Jackson: 'Two Contemporary Cults', *Advancement of Science* 23, June 1966, pp. 60–64.

21. This report which is highly critical of the practices of Scientology is not available for general circulation outside the State of Victoria, in Australia.

22. *Certainty*, Vol. 14, No. 3, 1967, p. 2.

23. See *The Auditor*, Nos. 23–27, 1967.

24. J. A. Jackson, *op. cit.*, pp. 60–63.

25. Richard Mathison, *God is a Millionaire*, New York: The Boestro-Merrill Co., 1960, p. 15.

6   'The Call': the Concept of Vocation in the Free Church Ministry

Eric Carlton

I

IN matters ministerial, Christians maintain that the prerogative rests with God. It is not man, but God who initiates action. ' . . . the Christian ministry . . . is not founded upon exceptional gifts, but upon the will of God. . . . In fact, almost anyone or anything may be used by God as the vehicle through which to confront an individual with His claim to obedience.' So reads *Concerning the Ministry*, a pamphlet issued by the Baptist Union for the benefit of those who are thinking of the ministry as their vocation. The writer, R. L. Child, Principal Emeritus of the Regent's Park College at Oxford, continues, 'But the vital thing is not how or when the call comes . . . it is that . . . when the decisive moment arrives, it finds us ready and waiting.' But, with some understatement, he admits that 'the constraint laid upon the heart and conscience, though deeply felt, may be hard to define'.

It is believed that this call is confirmed in four practical ways. Firstly, by the positive response of the candidate in seeking to equip himself for the service that lies ahead. The actual nature of the call may be in doubt. It it to the ministry as such, or to service along broader, more humanitarian lines? 'There is a place in His service for everyone who is willing to be used. But that place is not necessarily the ministry, for the ministry is not everyone's vocation. Hence the need of careful examination beforehand of what is involved.' But aspiring disciples find that really acceptable channels of service are few. Custom decrees that they at least investigate the possibility of theological college training, before other 'full-time service' avenues are explored.

Further confirmation of the genuineness of the call is seen in the applicant's qualifications. These qualifications are not primarily academic; spiritual conviction and moral integrity are looked for besides 'adequate intellectual equipment'. Additional reinforcement is supplied by the commendation of friends and the endorsement by the local church of the applicant's sense of vocation. Finally, the man's Ordination and Induction to a pastorate are believed to set the seal to the sanctifying process; he is now completely consecrated to the work of the Church.

Collar and Cloth, a booklet issued in 1963 by the British Council of Churches, has adopted a slightly off-key approach to the subject of ministerial vocation. The idealized picture of the parson here presented is that of the virile young sacramentalist who is both suitably humble and conveniently omniscient – an ecclesiastical Jack-of-all-trades who is in demand for his unique and indispensable services.

On most basic issues the literature is dogmatic and unanimous: the ministry can be a demanding business. The minister must be a student: this implies a capacity for sustained study of the Bible and other disciplines, and the power to communicate the fruits of his reading to others 'in ways that will arouse interest, challenge thought and nurture character'. His role, therefore, is that of the prophet who brings people the word of God, preaching and teaching, explaining and exhorting. A major responsibility of the Christian pastor is the 'care' of others. He must visit his people regularly – not just during the crises of life. He must know them intimately, listening and counselling, and even giving them practical help. In addition, he must organize the laity and guide its committees in order to make some impact upon the wider community. 'He needs to be a man deeply conscious of the value of human beings in the sight of God, and eager to manifest to old and young that genuine personal interest and loving concern which is the gift of Jesus Christ to His servants.' True to the spirit of the New Testament, the principles are enunciated, but the details of application are not worked out. Specific indications as to what to do in a given situation are rarely given, and may even be deemed unnecessary. In the true Protestant tradition, men – with God's help – must find their own way; variety of interpretation and freedom of action are integral to their faith.

Much of this literature is not so much vague as misleading. Vagueness there must be, since no writer is able to talk about 'inner realities' without recourse to abstractions. 'Call', 'guidance', 'salvation' – terms such as these must mean different things to different individuals. The tragedy seems to be that Christians now have them neatly categorized, whilst all the associated phenomena are conveniently standardized. So the intending minister interprets his call in terms of one of a limited number of stereotypes; the expected becomes the experienced.

Some of the literature is misleading in that the ministry is elevated to the position of the only true form of discipleship. This is rarely stated overtly, but the implication is clear. Passing – and merely perfunctory – references are made to the fact that all Christians can 'serve' whatever their occupations, but the inference that these are somehow less worthy is inescapable. The minister is the one who is *fully* committed; he is deemed to have 'chosen the better part'. This belief constitutes a very real pressure to the young aspirant, and it is exploited in the booklet by use of the 'challenge' approach. 'You may perhaps feel that such a vocation is beyond the power of any human being adequately to fulfil. If you do, you will be largely right. . . . Only God at least can supply what is needed . . . are you conscious that, in spite of natural shrinking, you have a desire, or feel an obligation, to serve Him in this way. . . .?' Or again, ' . . . many people throw away their talents and abilities enticed by the prospect of easy promotion and big money . . . what good are these things. . . .? How much wiser to choose work which you can enjoy to the full, which brings its own satisfaction and reward and stretches you to the limit . . . It is not for everyone, but it may be for you . . . There is no more absorbing and challenging work you can undertake.' Such an approach is not consonant with the egalitarian functionalism of Nonconformity; in fact, it is little short of spiritual extortion.

In a comparatively recent study of young Baptist ministers,[1] one unsurprising fact to emerge was that 'the call to the ministry' is particularly hard to define. Some described it as an inner restraint, a mounting and inescapable conviction that their future lies with the Church. This may persist over quite a long period of time, and efforts may be made to 'shake it off' or to rationalize it. Some men freely admitted that ideally they did not want to be ministers; that initially the idea repelled them, and that even now they are reluctant prophets. 'If you can forget about it, do', was the advice given to one hesitant candidate who contentedly shared a modest small-holding business with his father. It took him five years to decide; the step was ultimately precipitated by a crisis experience following the untimely death of a friend in the Forces. Only for a minority does the 'call' come suddenly. For them it may be a cataclysmic experience; an unsought revelation. But few lay claim to such an experience. For the majority, it is not entirely unexpected; it comes as a climax to a growing vocational awareness.

Opposition can be a negative form of encouragement. There is an attitude which holds that when the world condemns, God commends. For example, although none of the respondents in the Baptist study had been qualified professional men before entering the ministry, some were highly skilled tradesmen whose earning potential was considerable. There was the master baker who did not go to theological college until he was thirty-two,[2] and then only after a long period of indecision. Why not remain a layman? Even a prosperous layman can be a conscientious layman. Such a rationalization was obvious, and was therefore rejected as unworthy because it was felt to be no more than just that. Or again, the ex-RAF jet pilot who was a university-trained metallurgist,[3] desperately trying to maintain his multiplying family on a minimum stipend.[4] The prospects had been clear and promising, and were rejected – partly for that very reason. The need to deny oneself is part of the vocational concept – perhaps even central to religion itself – and cannot be satisfactorily explained as mere mental gratification, even though with some men it can become the stuff of self-pity.

Alternatively, the 'call' can take the form of vocational certainty born of conscious inadequacy. 'I couldn't speak in public, I couldn't lead in prayer – therefore I *knew* I was called!' Other men, with grave doubts, have resorted to the ultimatum approach. This simple consists of 'challenging God' to show clearly by some sign if the call is real. In these circumstances, it is possible hopefully to interpret even the faintly abnormal as a bolt from heaven. For example, the young man who 'sensed the answering presence of God' during a minor breakdown of his car; or another, who saw the ending of his youthful romance after a party as a sure indication of call.

The role of the aspirant's own mentors in the process – and particularly that of his own minister – varies considerably. Some take pains to channel the young man's enthusiasm along ministerial lines. His reading will then be 'guided'; and he may even be invited to the manse, feted, interrogated and eventually introduced to the perplexing maze of theological disputation. Almost certainly, he will be encouraged to widen the scope of his preaching from 'testimonies' at Christian Endeavour meetings to 'simple talks' at the unwanted women's meetings which his senior has reluctantly booked and now generously relinquishes in favour of his *protégé*. Some candidates, on the other hand, find their ministers rather cautious, even discouraging – though rarely uninterested. Young men sometimes have a rather romantic view of the ministry;[5] the senior man must guard against this, and against the natural tendency to mistake keenness for conviction. With so much apathy in the churches, it is understandable that a minister should over-indulge the young man who seems to be such promising ministerial material.

In the local church, especially if it is small and insignificant, the young enthusiast is always in demand. His modest attempts at what is narrowly yet ambitiously called 'Christian service', i.e. Sunday-school teaching, youth and witness team work, the occasional open-air testimony, etc., will be noted and even flattered. He will be referred to as a 'worker', 'keen' or possibly 'on fire for the Lord', depending upon the theological hue of the particular community in which he is being nurtured. Before long, a pattern of expectation concerning him will have formed, and this will constitute a gentle pressure which urges him towards full-time service. Many men are not conscious of such pressures; others do sense them and although some are resentful,[6] most appear to welcome their newly acquired status. For a while, they are big fish in little pools.

Ministers define their call in different ways; for simplicity of analysis, these may be termed particular and general. The majority feel themselves called to the specifically pastoral and preaching ministry.[7] There is something they want to tell, and they believe this is the best way of doing it. Others are not prepared to limit the precise nature of their call in this way. They emphasize that theirs is the service of God and man; it is broadly humanitarian as well as narrowly spiritual. Some admit that they would be as happy if they were Christian teachers or doctors, or serving society in some similar worthwhile capacity. It is usually the theologically liberal who do not see the human predicament in black-and-white terms, and who therefore tend to canalize their concern in humanitarian rather than ecclesiastical ways. Those, on the other hand, who experience an overpowering constraint to restrict their talents to the more conventional and acceptable service channels are usually largely drawn from the conservative ranks.[8]

The urge to evangelize is indigenous to the very ethos of theological conservatism. The awful judgement of God, the clear demarcation between the saved and the unsaved, the almost agonizing

concern for the 'lost', these are the generative forces which produce
the evangelical minister. For the earnest evangelical, life can be
hard and unrewarding in the 'world'. His opportunities for 'witness'
will be necessarily limited and perhaps, therefore, unimpressive.
Arguments with work-fellows are almost invariably inconclusive, and
the distinctiveness of his values may not be thrown into relief in the
ways he desires. The attitudes of people in offices and factories can
produce a near-violent reaction in the sensitive conservative; they
merely strengthen his conviction that they are wrong, and harden
his resolve to pursue an undeviating line. Such are the breeding
grounds for many a full-time candidate. Where compromise is
impossible, the ministry can almost be a retreat from the taunts and
indifference of the unconverted.

II
THE CALL TO THE LOCAL CHURCH

The minister, although assured of the divine nature of his call, is not
always sure how the fact of this call is to be made acceptable to others.
Theoretically, his necessarily subjective sense of commission is
objectively confirmed in the Act of Ordination,[9] and the subsequent
Induction to a local church. In these services, a church publicly
recognizes that the minister is consecrated to a God-appointed task,
although the relationship which is established between pastor and
people serves to qualify the nature of that recognition. It is in the
Induction Service that the history of the 'call' is recited, and the
minister-elect formally testifies to his sense of vocation. As T. H.
Spurgeon used to put it to his students, 'When you get out, you'll be
Ordained, Inducted and Recognized – one of them *has* to take'.

The 'call' to the local church, like the call to the ministry itself,
defies any very simple analysis. Ministers themselves often find it
extremely difficult to say precisely why they have chosen one church
and not another.[10] Sometimes, the church in which they happen to
have settled was the only one to give then a 'call' on this occasion.
But this is by no means always true; some men do – contrary to
in-group scepticism – turn down larger and more prosperous livings
to settle where they are.

It is customary for men to speak of 'challenge' and 'opportunity'
in relation to church settlements; these are the recurring themes. It
is obviously easy for a minister to rationalize the necessary accep-

tance of a humble, prospectless cause in terms of 'challenge'. Men have to settle somewhere, and a case must be made – particularly to one's fellow ministers – for the decision which is ultimately taken. There is some evidence that some men, especially the young and uninitiated who are still in the first throes of clerical courtship, over-confidently settle in low-state churches assuming the mantle of a personal deliverer. What others have not achieved, they will achieve. This is more characteristic of the conservatively minded who are assumed to be more generously endowed with charisma than their more liberal brethren, and who assume that 'blessing' must follow where 'the word is faithfully proclaimed'.

Not all men are so self-deceived; indeed, such an explanation might seem facile until one takes into account the deep-rooted attitudes inculcated in the ministerial candidate even before his formal training begins. 'Man's extremity is God's opportunity' is basic to his understanding of the divine method. The more inexplicable the event, the greater the challenge to a man's faith. The more impossible a thing appears to be, the more it is to be attempted. To champion, therefore, a seemingly hopeless cause, would seem infinitely more worthy to some men than to accept a position with a 'successful' church. But for many this is true only in so far as 'successful' churches lie outside their orbit.

Just what factors constitute a 'call'? Ministers talk of 'feeling right' on their first visit to a church, or when they 'preach with a view' to the pastorate and sense the response of the people. They may refer to what is nebulously termed 'atmosphere';[11] a man might well overlook all kinds of other more material deficiencies in a church, providing this intangible quality is present. The stipend, the membership, the manse, free Sundays, schools for the children – all these are important in any consideration of 'call', but ministers insist that these are externalities, and do not fully 'explain' *why* men make the decisions they do. They testify to hours spent in prayer, and may Mosaically look for a few modest 'signs', disregarding the dangers of self-congratulatory fulfilments.

In the Baptist study, the majority of those interviewed believed that God does call a man to a specific church. To insist upon this as an inviolable rule raises insuperable difficulties. The facts just do not support this; unsatisfactory settlements are obviously made and innumerable men leave churches under some kind of recriminatory cloud. This situation cannot be explained away by high-sounding references to 'the economy of God' (with the suggestion that it was pre-ordained that we should learn from these particular mistakes); this is merely to slide out by a convenient theological back-door. A minority insisted that the call to serve is a general one, and that within reason one church is as good as another. It is simply a matter of availability, opportunity and suitability. All men were asked whether in view of the known abuses of 'call' terminology and the 'call' system, it might not be better to substitute the term 'invitation', which has a very different connotation. Many equivocated about this. When pressed for a reply in both particular and general senses, the vast majority (77%) believed that *they* had been specifically called to their own churches, but doubted if this were generally true of others!

A man is said to be fitted for the ministry primarily by his sense of vocation. The socio-psychological preconditions which help to determine the call are interesting, and the ways in which it is subsequently channelled in settlements that are made, broken and justified poses disturbing questions for the committed Nonconformist. The language that tends to constitute a pressure on the pre-college candidate is the language he in turn employs to explain the nature and purpose of his actions. Terminology such as 'salvation', 'guidance' and 'call' is associational, evocative and even coercive. This is the language which can blur social realities, that can appear to explain the inexplicable and inspire the indefensible. The anomalies are not entirely unrecognized; the concept of the 'call' in the Free Church ministry is an intriguing study in institutionalized ambiguity.

NOTES

1. E. Carlton, *The Probationer Minister: A Study among English Baptists*, M.Sc.(Econ.) thesis, University of London, 1965.

2. Note the unofficial college dictum that ideally candidates should be 'about twenty-two and unmarried'. Strange (but practical?) limits for a denomination in which it is held that the Holy Spirit cannot be unresistingly harnessed by ritual formulae or by ecclesiastical necessity.

3. A sample of 50 was selected in a statistical population of 152, of which 67 were graduates, 19 with non-theological degrees.

4. At this time, £520 per annum, with an additional £40 for the first child and £15 each for all subsequent children.

5. In the Baptist sample, only 17% were sons of deacons, and only one respondent was a minister's son. This is something of a reversal of the inter-war trend. It would appear that those from families which are closely connected with church

administration often become disenchanted with the concept of ministerial vocation.

6. 'My parents were thrilled at the prospect of the ministry, but I detested the idea originally', said one Baptist probationer with a Salvation Army background.

7. Some respondents claimed to have had this conviction from youth. 'I have always known it – though the call came in a special way when I was 15.'

8. In the Baptist study, 75 % of the sample claimed to be strongly conservative before entering college, 63 % (i.e. 80 % of the original number) still maintained an 'informed conservative' approach in the ministry.

9. Although Nonconformist ministers, in general, regard Ordination as binding and ostensibly permanent, and tend to repudiate the 'indelible orders' of their Anglican counterparts, the alarming rate of ministerial wastage shows how flexibly this can be interpreted. See Bryan Wilson, *Religion in Secular Society*, London: Watts, 1966, p. 80.

10. That the choice is really free at all is questioned by some. A superintendent minister's wishes can assume the force of a directive, and there are other factors which may weigh in favour of a particular response in given situations.

11. This is very real to those concerned; where the necessary psychological preconditions are present, 'a spirit of expectancy' is generated, and this together with the effective rapport achieved between preacher and people constitutes 'atmosphere'.

7 Catholic, Evangelical and Liberal in the Anglican Priesthood

Michael Daniel

THE clergy of the Church of England, as well as our politicians and economists, find themselves midway between the Common Market and the United States. They are less honoured than in America, and less rejected than on the Continent. They are neglected. In America they top the prestige charts, and many clergy when describing their work refer to the minister's high job-satisfaction.[1] On the Continent anticlericalism is a general attitude in many industrial cities, and sometimes *'salaud'* and *'chrétien'* are interchangeable words.[2]

These opposite experiences would appear to account quite adequately for the prevailing clergy attitudes towards the society in which they work. In America the clergy of the mainstream churches are noted for their accommodation to the prevailing social values. Protestantism, Catholicism, and Judaism are but sub-divisions of the prevailing religion, 'Protestant–Catholic–Jewish'[3] whose main content and practice is a glorification of the American way of life. They are said to preach, typically, uplift sermons, and hesitate to criticize the prevailing norms,[4] lest they be rejected, and possibly dismissed from an agreeable and well-paid job.

In many industrial cities of Western Europe, on the other hand, the clergy have several generations' experience of rejection by manual workers and by many intellectuals,[5] and this is leading to a counter-attack by the clergy against powers of secular thought and religious apathy. They tend to view themselves as missionaries in hostile territory and seek to gain converts to train as lay shock-troops. Persecution is turned to a positive good, it encourages heroism, the heroic band of loving brethren who hate the powers of darkness while loving those whom they seek to win, as in the early days of Christianity, of Methodism, and of Socialism.

Neglect brings no reward. The English clergy get neither pleasure from being appreciated, nor stimulation from attack, nor even much notice; only a humorous tolerance, except when needed for *rites de passages*, when temporary but earnest gravity is donned as a mask. What response is possible to this situation?

I suggest that the response to honour in America – accommodation – involves primarily a change in goals towards which the clergyman is aiming. His sermon remains the same in form, but the values it promotes are conformity to this-worldly values. The pastoral pattern may be modified to become the new counsellor relationship, as church secondary relationships succeed the primary ones possible in the smaller congregation. But this is not important here. What counts is that the counsellor relationship of the clergyman is used more to promote the client's successful integration into the world as it is than to direct him towards a more perfect way. The response to rejection on the Continent, on the other hand, is not a change of goals but a change of means. For instance, the parish system may be seen as a failure in the context of an unchurched urban *zone humaine*, and so is replaced, while the aim to redeem and sanctify both the individual and society is in no way changed or even redefined. Confidence is undiminished. Only appropriate means and greater efforts are required.[6]

Rejection at least produces an impact and a response. Neglect produces nothing but anxiety. If Christianity is important to just a few of us while all the rest are friendly and willing, but just can't see the point, isn't it probable that we are simply deluded and are making a fuss about nothing? Withdrawal into the little world of the faithful but uninspired remnant is hardly practicable for the family clergyman in the city. He is goaded by anxiety into questioning either his goals, or the means he is using to attain his goals, or both. This is, of course, a very general picture. Many factors may operate to change the situation, though each in only a minority of cases. An annulus of suburbs at a certain distance round London is spoken of as the 'Bible belt', and here the pattern is an attenuated replica of the American suburb drawn in cartoon by W. H. Whyte in *The Organization Man*. Areas where there is rivalry between Catholics and Protestants may show external signs of a competitive vitality, as in the Whit Walks, where the many who rarely worship still parade. Whether people 'really' tend to be less religious nowadays than they used to be is not the point here. It is simply that most of them don't seem to need the parson or his message any more, and so he may often experience a deep anxiety (even if he tries to hide it from himself) as to whether perhaps he has got it all wrong.

In this situation, I suggest, he has two alternatives. He may redefine his beliefs and so change his operational goals, or he may change the means to attain his goals – or both. Actually this is an over-simplification. He may redefine his own beliefs so radically that he dare not admit having done so, and he is then faced with having to go through the motions of helping others to attain goals which he has altered almost beyond recognition for himself, in order not to upset the beliefs they have and probably could not change. For instance, some clergy reject a belief in 'the life of the world to come' and yet are obliged to continue preaching the scriptures in the conventional terms, comforting the bereaved and aged with the promise of reunion and a life from which pain has been removed. These may only admit their redefinitions to a very few individuals whom they can trust, and usually to no one in their parishes. This problem is one that I do not propose to follow any further, since I am more concerned with the question as to which alternative a clergyman will choose – whether he will redefine his beliefs and so change his goals (overtly or covertly), or whether he will maintain intact his already established beliefs and modify his means in an attempt to persuade others to seek the goals – or either, or both. The full range of choices is that he might retain his goals and his means unchanged; retain his goals and change his means; change his goals and retain the original means; or change both goals and means.

Empirical evidence

There is some evidence that the factor determining which alternative a clergyman will choose is the particular religious ideology which he already holds – that nexus of beliefs and interpretations which in the Church of England is called 'churchmanship'. This concept is worth discussion before the behavioural choices are discussed.

When clergy are asked where they stand in this matter – how they would label themselves, most reply with some reference to a polarity which is variously described as Catholic/evangelical or high church/evangelical. Many men who put themselves near one pole will not be sensitive to the nuances which exist near to the other. The Catholic may confuse evangelical with low, which refers usually to an unenthusiastic and unsacramental traditionalism. The evangelical is less to blame in confusing the Catholic with the self-styled high church man since the difference tends to be negligible in many cases; but where it exists it usually refers to the individual's position in the controversy between the Roman and Anglican churches and their ministries. For our present purposes we can ignore such subtleties, particularly as in many cases the label a clergyman adopts is strongly influenced by the tradition of the parish he serves, or the church background he comes from.

It would be reasonable to assume that both the uncompromising Catholic and evangelical would be equally committed to a maintenance of their established norms both as to goals and means. At least there are no *a priori* grounds for expecting a difference. The rigidity with which fundamental values are defended may be expected to overflow into an equally rigid defence of the means which have been traditionally used to attain them, well beyond the value with which tradition, or dogma, have already endowed them. Yet the evidence, at least of the London area, does not bear this out.

It is true that the most extreme or uncompromising Catholics and evangelicals do not differ very much in their modifications of the means they have traditionally used. The Catholic's insistence on the use of as many of the sacraments as possible is only a little more rigid than the evangelical's insistence on the emotion-generated psychological crisis and the precisely placed conversion. Yet the latter tends to state clearly that although he is a conservative evangelical in his interpretation of the Bible and God's Word and in his certainty of salvation, he is a liberal as regards the means by which these values may be offered and accepted. He stresses his flexibility, and states that he is searching for new ways to present Christ and to win others for him. So the conservative Catholic tends to maintain both his goals and means unchanged, while the conservative evangelical tends to maintain his goals but be ready to change his means a little.

The liberals[7] of either wing tend to differ from one another more remarkably. The man who calls himself a liberal evangelical, or uses some similar label, varies little from his conservative counterpart. He appears more open in his range of interests, especially in other ideologies, but fundamentally his goals are as fixed as the others; he is only more liberal in the extent to which he will modify his means. He may even play bingo. The liberal Catholic, on the other hand, tends to be fairly conservative in that he stresses the sacraments and other means, while redefining the goals. He is becoming more this-worldly in general orientation, more concerned with the successful integration of the individual into the society of this world, less with his being numbered among the society of the next. He is, in fact, fairly close to one modal position of those clergy who do not describe themselves as Catholics, evangelicals, or by any near equivalent of those terms. I am not, at the moment, meaning those who call themselves central, for this usually indicates a conservative, if not an old-fashioned hold to both means and goals (this is the other mode), but to those who frequently object to allowing any label at all to be tied to them. They feel themselves to be individuals in their way of interpreting what they believe and do.

Let me begin to illustrate (if not always to support) my contentions by introducing a few research findings more explicitly. A very few simply call themselves liberals, but most will hunt around for a combination of words which could adequately describe their position and are unsatisfied with whatever formulation they produce. One cited his own name, and said that that was the only label he could accept as describing his position; another evaded any labelling by saying that any type-casting is inadequate.

These are the clergy who tend most to a radical redefinition of beliefs and goals and of the means appropriate to attaining them. Yet by virtue of being members of a centralized and bureaucratic church they are not free to express their changes as radically as they would like. They are most rigidly bound by the means appointed for them, as they are required to perform certain religious services and duties by diocesan authority which can impose sanctions quite effectively through holding the purse-strings. But bishops will avoid the scandal of action over heresy if they can, and while the clergyman may not officially publish his beliefs (except negatively by what he leaves out of his sermons), he will discuss his views quite freely with friends. 'Completely existential' is a phrase one man used to describe his position. Another did not regard the Trinity as composed of persons, although God was 'personal' in a metaphysical sense. Another definitely discounted any sort of future life.

The difference in attitude to fundamental beliefs, between the Catholic group, the evangelical group, and the group that contains all the other clergymen, which one might designate 'other', can be aptly illustrated by their reactions to the Bishop of Woolwich's bestseller *Honest to God*.[8] It was in this book that most clergy first came face to face with the radical reinterpretations of traditional dogma associated with the continental theologians Bultmann, Bonhoeffer, and Tillich. Nine-tenths of them had read it; but only a twentieth of the evangelicals viewed it favourably, while a quarter of the Catholics and two-thirds of all the others did.

A most interesting characteristic of this 'other' group of clergy is that although they accept neither Catholic nor evangelical as descriptive epithets, they almost all show unmistakable signs of a Catholic past. Two specific criteria were used to test this impression; the theological college at which a man had been trained, and the type of principal Sunday morning service at the church where he served. Only four had been at a more or less evangelical college, while eighteen had been at what might be loosely described as Catholic ones. One was at a church which used a non-sacramental type of main Sunday service, while eighteen were at churches which called the main service Holy Communion, Eucharist, or Mass. No doubt there are more Catholic clergymen than evangelical ones in the population at risk, but the proportions are nothing like so disparate. The chance is remote that these slender figures, or the more weighty body of impressions gained in talking to the clergy, are just due to random sampling.

Liberals

Nearly half the clergy thought that they were, theologically speaking, conservatives, while almost a third thought that they were theologically liberals. Nevertheless, more than half said that they had become more liberal than they were a few years ago, and only less than a fifth said they had moved the other way. Most of the conservatives had become more liberal, and so had most of the liberals, but a few of both groups had moved the other way; though, as I said before, among the conservative evangelicals any move towards liberalism was evident in means rather than in goals. The reasons for this trend towards liberalism are speculative, but are probably connected with the ideological overtones of the word itself in England, as in America and most of western Europe. Individual freedom is a much-prized value in many areas of our culture. The term is also used as a correlative of 'progressive', and many clergy wish to be thought go-ahead and energetic in a society which is basically competitive, and in which the church has been thought to be lagging.

It is more interesting to speculate on why the group of clergy who *behave* like liberals, and who do not accept Catholic or evangelical (or equivalent) labels, should appear to have arrived from the Catholic camp, or at least from among its camp-followers. I have a strong impression that the evangelicals have an element of combativeness, of the need for conflict, built into their definition of the Christian situation. This does not appear to be the same attitude as that held by Weber's 'bearer of the Protestant ethic'. The individual Christian is not the man to whom the world and its people appear as an impersonal environment in which he is to labour at his calling to find signs of his election. Rather the evangelical clergyman is a man who can afford a measure of humour, and who loves his fellow man with warmth even while hating the powers of this world which have ensnared him. The evangelical clergyman expects to engage in conflict with the person whom he seeks to win for Christ, and this shows in the challenging eye and tone of voice and the way in which he turns the conversation on to the central topic of decision for Christ. All this takes place on the individual confrontation level.

In this way the evangelical is able to interpret neglect as rejection, for in every case of neglect which he can enter into on a personal level of confrontation with the neglecter, he can force an implicit demand for decision. If the neglect then continues, this is tantamount to rejection. That the challenge has not been sufficiently comprehended to make a decision a real possibility is not usually considered. The response the evangelical clergyman makes to this experienced rejection of his challenge can then be similar to that rejection which the continental priest experiences both of his faith and of himself. Rejection produces zest and heroism.

The Catholic clergyman in the Church of England is at a disadvantage here. He is primarily concerned with membership of the visible Church of Christ, and since most of the individuals he meets in the pastoral situation have been baptized in infancy he cannot view them primarily as outsiders with whom he has a basic conflict relationship. Pastoral is the operative word. They are sheep whom he must shepherd and nourish, and in so far as the image influences the experienced situation, he becomes less able to struggle with recalcitrant members. One doesn't expect to fight with sheep; one either leads them or drives them. Elements of this difference were clearly visible in discussion with clergy about how they viewed their work. Two-fifths of the Catholics said that they were irritated by their lay people. None of the evangelicals did. Several evangelicals cited 'ruthlessness' as a desirable characteristic for a clergyman to have in pursuing his ministry – none of the Catholics did. Nearly half the Catholics cited holiness, calmness or serenity, as qualities in clergymen who had influenced them; only a quarter of the evangelicals did. A third of the evangelicals criticized 'uncommittedness' in other clergy; only an eighth of the Catholics did. Even though statistical significance at the 95% level was sometimes attained for pointers like these, they must remain no more than straws to indicate a prevailing tendency. Statistical significance cannot indicate any significance on the level of meaning. Nevertheless, these little pointers are worth giving as examples of evidence gained in conversations with clergy, which can be considerable in aggregate.

The self-image of the Catholic clergyman may well be a fragile thing in the present atmosphere of neglect. Neglect cannot easily be interpreted as rejection and so be responded to with vigour, and the Catholic church on earth has been a static and authoritarian body which cannot easily attract kudos by a dusting of progressive liberalism. He searches for a more reassuring and viable self-image, and finds it in a measure of theological liberalism, which agrees with the prevailing values of our secular culture. But this attitude is not easily reconcilable with either the goals or the means of traditional Catholicism, and his attachment to this is weakened. This may, at least in part, explain why the majority of those who are reluctant to accept traditional labels, and whose thinking and behaviour are in harmony with this reluctance, have reached this position from a Catholic background rather than an evangelical one.

NOTES

1. These remarks about American clergy are applicable only to urban mainstream churches.

2. Quoted by a worker-priest. See D. L. Edwards (ed.), *Priests and Workers: an Anglo-French Discussion*, London: SCM Press, 1961.

3. W. Herberg, *Protestant, Catholic, Jew*, New York: Doubleday, 1960.

4. P. Berger, *The Noise of Solemn Assemblies*, New York: Doubleday, 1961. E. Q. Campbell and T. F. Pettigrew, *Christians in Racial Crisis*, Washington D.C.: Public Affairs Press, 1959.

5. Witness, for instance, the considerable literature on the worker-priests and the Mission à France, and also the work of the Protestant 'lay academies'.

6. Naturally this is a broad generalization. Exceptions can be cited. Some clergy plod on with the traditional parish congregation of a few elderly people and small children. A few radically redefine their beliefs and goals.

7. Empirical evidence cited in this article is based on research into a stratified random sample of 95 clergymen in the Greater London Council area who were ordained between 1955 and 1965. It is more fully described in a London M.Phil. thesis dated 1967, entitled *London Clergymen*.

8. London: SCM Press, 1963.

8 An Analysis of the Effectiveness of Methodist Churches of Varying Sizes and Types in the Liverpool District

Frank Pagden

INTRODUCTION

THIS INVESTIGATION began when it was noticed that while the
total numbers of Methodist members in the country was dropping
year by year, the Liverpool District's numbers were rising, and had
been going up almost every year since 1942. As the Liverpool
District, though compact in size, is made up of about 25,000 members living in city, suburban, rural, and industrial circuits, it was
difficult to pin down any obvious reason for its success.

The questions and enquiries from the Connexional and District
Church Membership Committees encouraged us to try to isolate the
reason.

Transfers. At first, the possibility that the district had gained from
members transferred into it from other districts was looked at. It was
found that far from benefitting from transfers, in fact the District
lost considerably in most years. Apart from 1957, when the district
gained 650 members in the realignment of District boundaries, there
was a loss shown every year on transfer of membership. This loss was
severe from 1932 to 1942, when it averaged over 250 each year.
From 1942 to 1962, the loss averaged about 100 members, and from
1963 to 1966, it averaged about 200 members. The gain in total
membership was not because of transfers of members, but in spite of it.

Deaths and 'Ceased to Meet'. The death-rate and the 'Ceased to
Meet' figures were very near to the average for the whole of Methodism, and could not have been responsible for the rise in numbers.
One interesting fact emerged from these charts, however. Though
the deaths of Methodists during the war years on Merseyside

showed no increase above average, the 'Ceased to Meet' chart shows a very high number, double the usual number, crossed off during 1941. Were these men and women the spiritual casualties of those years?

New Members. It is when one looks at the figure for new members received that the cause of Liverpool's rise becomes obvious. From 1946–63, the Liverpool District has been receiving an average of about 4·4 new members per year, for every 100 people in membership at the beginning of the year. This contrasts sharply with the average throughout Methodism, which is close to 3·5% for that period. It is known that Methodism loses around 4% of its membership every year from all causes. It can be said with confidence, that providing the transfer situation of members equalizes itself, if a church, circuit or District receives more than 4% new members per year, it will grow. If it receives less, it will decline in total numbers. Of course, annual losses vary a little from year to year, and place to place, but on the whole the 4% new members is a good general guide with which to forecast future trends.

Since 1963 the Liverpool District's 'productivity' of new members has dropped below 4% for the first time for seventeen years, and caused the first pronounced drop in total numbers for many years. The Liverpool District graphs show clearly that there is a relation between the figure of 4% new members and whether the total goes up or down.

What is success? One cannot say that the 'productivity figure' of new members is a complete guide to the 'success' of a church, for some small churches are very outgoing and obedient to the Spirit of God, and some larger ones could be so involved in 'counting heads' in a social club way as to be spiritually dead. Even so, it can be said that a live church, which is trying to live and proclaim the Gospel, is bound to show the effects of this either soon or late, by gaining new members. To ask 'How many new members have each hundred of you won this year?' is as acid a test as our available statistics enable us to make.

All the work that was done so far had succeeded in isolating the fact that the Liverpool totals had risen because the new members exceeded the 'break-even' norm of 4%. This merely pushed the question further back, and one had to ask 'Why does Liverpool make more new members than the average in Methodism?'

Starting Points. Many people with long experience in Methodist administration suggested various causes, but none of them could be immediately checked, as there was no hard evidence for any of them. Two points seemed promising. Over some years past, the Liverpool District has tackled the thorny problems of redundancy and redevelopment with energy and determination, especially in the inner-belt city areas. Was this the cause? Was it because old buildings had been demolished and new ones built of a viable size and in strategic areas?

Another theory seemed promising, too. This was the idea that Liverpool had many churches of about 200 membership, which is an efficient size, evangelically speaking. Both of these points, linked as they are, provided a good starting point.

District Figures. In order to find out if the size of a Methodist Society had any relation to its 'productivity' of new members, the first work was done on District level, using the annual schedules printed in the Minutes of Conference, 1960–63. The Districts were put in a list in order of 'productivity', Liverpool at the top with 4·34%, down to South Wales at the bottom with 1·35%. Alongside the list was put the average number of members per society in each District. As the average number of members per society throughout Methodism in 1963, was 64, all Districts with over the 64 average were shaded on the chart. It was then seen clearly that of the ten most productive Districts at the top of the chart, all but one had more than 64 members per Society. Of the ten least productive at the bottom of the chart, all but one had less than 64 members per Society. Liverpool itself was the most productive, and with an average 141 members per Society was well ahead of the others. Thus it seemed that there may well be some sort of relation between the two things.

A District, however, is a big unit, and while promising, these figures could not be relied on.

Circuit Figures. Work was then done on circuit figures. Taking the figures for 1960–63 for the twenty-two circuits of the Liverpool Districts, the same type of chart was made. As the average number of members per society was 141 in Liverpool District, all circuits with more than 141 were shaded. An interesting picture developed. The eleven most productive circuits showed average memberships of between 153 and 221 members per society. The eleven less productive circuits showed either less than 132 members or more than 251! Thus we seemed to be on the way to proving that the bigger the church, the more effective it is. But this seemed to be true only of churches up to a certain size, about 250 members, above that, efficiency drops off.

These figures were then plotted on to a graph, a line drawn round the outermost plots and shaded in. The result showed a definite curve as below.

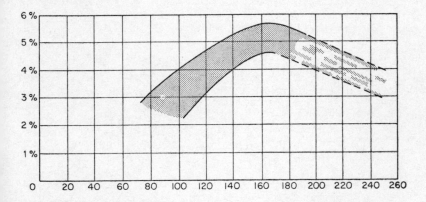

Thus it seemed that the most productive size of church was between 140 and 180 members. But even more promising as this graph was, over the District figures, weight could not be put on the findings, for it had two major flaws.

1. It was made up from finding the mean average of churches in a circuit. As many circuits have societies of 300 and of 30 members, averaging such a wide variation could be misleading.
2. As there were only two circuits in the district averaging over 200 members per society, the sample was too small to make any conclusion worthwhile about them.

Society Survey – Difficulties and Decisions. So it seemed that no reliable findings could be quoted until statistics for a large number of individual societies were obtained. Another factor emerged too. Even with district and circuit figures, we were on the way to proving that there was a relation between productivity of new members and size of society, but we had not shown that there was any *causal* relationship. Somehow, we had to find a way of demonstrating that the size of the society was a *cause* of good 'productivity' of new members.

When this kind of research is attempted, one comes up against the lack of statistical records in Methodism, and the lack of a record office where these figures are assembled together. The best way of showing a causal relationship is to take as wide a survey as possible over many different types of society, and to do it personally by getting in touch with them every December for a period of years. This was not practical for us, so the following procedure was adopted.

1. As the Liverpool District is itself a wide mixture of types of Church, urban, city, industrial, rural, etc., the survey was limited to the District itself. Many of the circuits did not have strong connections with Liverpool culturally, but looked to other surrounding towns, Preston, Wigan, Chester, etc.

2. With the agreement of the District Redevelopment Commission, extra questions were added to one of their schedules and sent to Circuit Superintendents. Two of the Superintendents did not give the details required, but 20 did.

3. Ideally, the productivity of a church would be worked out by dividing the number of new members at the end of a year into the total membership at the beginning of the year for three years running, and averaging the results. However, in order to make it easier for the Superintendents, we asked for the number of new members in each of the previous three years (1963, 1964 and 1965) and the total membership per society at the end of that period. This meant some inaccuracy in the final figures, but it was felt that as all the figures would be treated in the same way, for a large number of societies, these errors would largely cancel each other out. Thus it was decided that this amount of 'tolerance' was acceptable.

It was expected that the results when plotted on a graph would conform to a wedge-shaped pattern. In the case of small societies, a small group of new members might be received in one year, and then several years might elapse before others are received. In this case, the 'productivity' figure, averaged over three years might be very high or very low. (In fact one society, Moss Lane, with seven members, received one new member in 1964, and on the strength of that reached a productivity figure of 4·8%!) It could be expected that the plots on the graph for small societies would be widely spread, but that as larger societies were covered, the lots should get closer. Hence it was expected that this wedge-shaped pattern should be seen. The interesting factor was whether this wedge would point above the norm of 4% or below. If it pointed above 4%, it would seem that the larger societies were more efficient, and that we could adopt the simple rule 'The Bigger the Better'.

But, in fact, when the plots were completed, the wedge showed clearly pointing towards 3% at the sharp end. No clear lessons could be drawn from this, so more work was done on the plots themselves.

First, the productivity of all churches whose membership stood at 0-19, 20-39, 40-59, etc., was averaged, and a productivity line was drawn. There were too few churches with between 280 and 340 members to make it possible to cover these, but the others showed a clear pattern, as below:

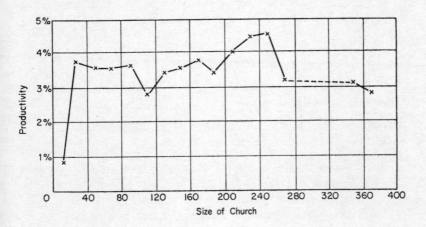

It will be seen that the productivity of churches below 20 is very small (0·9%), that churches from 20-100 strong do quite well (average 3·6%), from 100-200 not quite so well (average 3·5%), but from 200-60, productivity rises dramatically to 4·5%, thereafter it drops. The dotted line shows a lack of churches from 280-340 membership, until a group of three churches 340-60 membership show 3·1%, 360-80 members show 2·8%.

E

To get a more even line, and bigger groupings, especially of the large churches, the same plots were grouped in forties.

Members	Churches	Average productivity
0–39	16	3·03%
40–79	32	3·54%
80–119	23	3·3%
120–159	21	3·45%
160–199	15	3·48%
200–239	10	4·27%
240–279	8	3·8%
280–319	3	(2·53%)
320–359	3	(3·07%)
360–400	7	3·23%

Note: The percentages in brackets were considered to be based on inadequate evidence. Not included in these averages were churches in exceptional situations, i.e. one joint Anglican/Methodist Church, churches with attached schools or colleges, and city missions.

This appears to show that on the average, the most productive size of church is between 200 and 260 members strong.

BREAKDOWN OF THE GRAPH

With this graph it is possible to go into greater detail than with either district or circuit graphs.

Stewardship. The thirty-two churches in the District who had embarked on Stewardship programmes before 1963 were isolated.

Three were seriously below the average productivity (more than 1% below).
Eight were a little below the average (within 1% below).
Eight were a little above the average (within 1% above).
Thirteen were considerably above average (more than 1% above).

This encourages the belief that there is a link between stewardship and success in gaining new members.

City Churches. Thirty-six of the churches were described as 'city', being either in the inner belt of Liverpool or at the older end of large towns. Apart from five, of above 340 members, whose productivity varied from 1·5% to 5·8%, nearly all of the others fell into three groups.

1. Of churches with *40–100* members, four show low figures (0·6%–2·8%).
2. Also with *40–100* members, there is a close group of seven churches showing high figures (5·0%–6·4%). Thus it raises the question as to what additional factors are involved here. As both groups are made up of churches from different circuits, further research might well provide fruitful guidelines for city work in similar units.
3. Of churches with *100–240* members, few of the fifteen were holding their own, only five being above 4%. They seem to be averaging about 3·5% which is the district average.

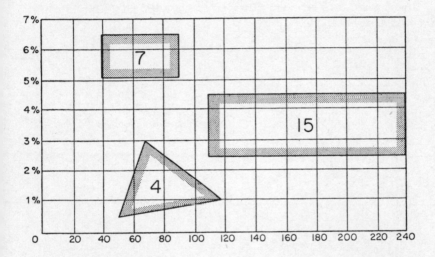

Conclusion. It appears that larger churches in cities are finding the going tough, but that smaller societies can thrive. To find out *how* needs more research.

Rural Churches. Thirty-seven of the churches were described as 'rural'. This included both village churches, and those in small country towns. It is very difficult to discern any real pattern about their work. The size of society does not seem to affect their productivity of new members. Fifteen churches showed figures of over 4% and these churches were from seven members to the top limit of 150 members. Those which showed less than 4% productivity were equally scattered.

Most of these societies were from 30 to 90 members strong and showed figures of between 3% and 5%, in a scattered way.

The most interesting point about the rural graph is that the figures suddenly slump, when the societies get below 30 members strong. Only three showed any new members at all; seven sent in a 'nil' return. It would seem, therefore, that once a rural church gets below 30 membership, the chances are that its days are numbered.

Suburban Churches. Fifty-seven of the churches in the district are classed as 'suburban'. These showed a quite distinct productivity curve. The smaller churches are less effective, and effectiveness rises to a peak when churches are 200 to 280 membership, and drops from then on. The edges of the pattern on the graph were distinct and were as below.

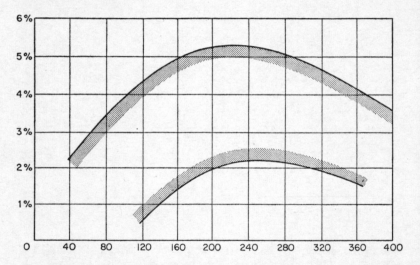

New Area Churches. Twenty-seven of the churches were in new areas, or were older churches with substantial new development adjoining. The graph plots showed a widely varying scatter of results. Some small societies showed small results, others showed very good results. There was no clear pattern. Thirteen of the churches showed less than 4% new members, while the other fourteen showed more than 4%. Size did not seem to be an important factor in new areas.

The interesting point is that, as a whole, the new area churches showed better results than the District average. As this study is based on new members only and takes no account of transfer of members, this is a surprising result, compared with the generally held view that new areas are tough to work.

It seems that here is a fruitful field for more research. The further breakdown of these figures, and a survey of these churches may well isolate the things that made for effectiveness.

CONCLUSIONS

The greatest service that this sort of enquiry can do, is to assist the policy-makers of Methodism in asking the right questions.

That this is an important and valuable field of study is becoming more obvious. The vast amount of the church's resources spent on new building, amalgamation and rebuilding, and the worrying decisions that face so many District Redevelopment Commissions, mean that those who are responsible for big decisions should have as much relevant information as possible in their hands. If this type of research makes it possible to spend more usefully, and judge more wisely, it will have been worthwhile.

The question which this enquiry set out to answer was, 'Does the size of the church affect its effectiveness?' It seems to do so in suburban areas. It appears that Methodism is so organized that it works best in suburban areas when the churches are between 200 and 280 members strong. Below this, there is possibly more worry about buildings and offices held, and less time can be devoted to evangelism. In addition, smaller churches have less of a minister's time, and this could affect their work. Above 280 members, the effectiveness seems to decrease. This could be due to the task being too much for the minister or 'half-minister' allocated to the church. It could be due to a lessening of the sense of 'community' which should characterize a live church. Or it could be that larger churches tend to accumulate more nominal members, who make no real contribution.

Although the work has been done on the basic size of the society, some sample work was done on ministerial manpower to see how this affected the productivity of new members. Enough work was done to show that there was a close parallel between the two things. The larger the society, the more of a minister's time they had. A fruitful avenue of work would be to see if there is a level of staffing which produces the best results, and what it is. This would involve enquiry into modern management techniques, and could be most helpful.

Interesting as the present results are, it becomes obvious that much more work is needed on the sociology of church life. The results of the enquiry into new areas, and cities in particular, point to the need for work beyond the capability of busy ministers, both in time and skill.

9 Religious Census of Bishop's Stortford

Anthony Spencer

INTRODUCTION

IN SEPTEMBER 1965 Socio-Religious Research Services (SRRS) launched an Ecumenical Census Service. The service offered either a 'major' or a 'minor' census to any Council of Churches or similar group interested. These had the double objective of social action and the establishment of an information system for the churches co-operating. The social action takes the form of a deliberate structured attempt to raise the level of neighbourly concern and co-operation, and so reduce isolation, loneliness and calls on the welfare services. The information system works through the network of 'way-warden' teams that provides the structure of the social action programme. These way-wardens pass on to the registrars of their respective churches information about the movement of population, so that the standardized church records can be kept up to date. The function of the census itself is twofold: to establish the initial records, on the basis of a card for each household, and to provide the training and motivation for the social action programme. As a by-product there is obtained data about the religious composition of the population. This article offers a preliminary analysis of the by-product of the Bishop's Stortford census, which was undertaken in autumn 1966.

Social and Cultural Background

Bishop's Stortford is an Urban District with a population of 20,830 in mid-1966.[1] The population has been rising since World War II; it was 12,772 at the 1951 Census, and 18,308 in 1961. The town lies in Hertfordshire, 31 miles to the north of London. There is a good train service into Liverpool Street, the journey taking 45 minutes, and many who live at Bishop's Stortford commute daily into London.

SAMPLE

The data used for this article was derived from a 10% random sample of the household cards completed during the census, stratified by street or road within district. This sample produced 620 cards, of which one was devoid of detail. The remaining 619 cards gave brief details of 1,892 persons. This suggests an overall coverage of over 90% of the population. In the analysis which follows special attention will be given to the religious homogeneity of household as this is a subject on which little published data is available.

Religious affiliation of the whole population

The instructions given to enumerators regarding the completion of the card included (*inter alia*) the following points:

> Where the household are all members of the same family (including 'in-laws') any of its adult members can complete the card for the others. But if the household includes an adult who is not a member of the family, he she should be asked to state his own Christian name and religion. If such a person is out at the time of your call, you should arrange to call again later to see him, unless the head of the household is quite positive about his religion, e.g. 'He goes to Mass every Sunday at the Roman Catholic Church'. When people with different surnames live at the same address, make sure that you enquire about each one, particularly when it is clear that lodgers are taken.

The religious affiliation of the 1892 people in the sample is given in Table 1 below.

Table 1   RELIGIOUS COMPOSITION OF HOUSEHOLD MEMBERS

	No.	%
Anglican, Church of England	1,409	74·4
Baptist	57	3·0
Congregationalist	64	3·4
Methodist	58	3·1
Presbyterian	11	0·6
Quaker	—	—
Roman Catholic	188	10·0
Salvation Army	11	0·6
Unitarian	1	—
Other religion	22	1·2
Atheist, agnostic, humanist, rationalist, etc.	52	2·7
Not stated	19	1·0
	1,892	100·0

Age and Religious Affiliation

One column on the household card asked for the year of birth of those under 21. By implication, all persons with no entry in this column were 21 or over. Table 2 gives a broad age analysis on this footing. (Percentages based on totals under 25 are not shown.)

Table 2 ADULTS AND MINORS IN SAMPLE
OF HOUSEHOLD MEMBERS

	Adults		Minors		Minors as % of
	No.	%	No.	%	Total Affiliation
Anglican, Church of England	965	74·5	444	74·4	31·5
Baptist	42	3·2	15	2·5	26·3
Congregationalist	45	3·5	19	3·2	29·6
Methodist	40	3·1	18	3·0	31·0
Presbyterian	9	0·7	2	0·3	—
Roman Catholic	111	8·6	77	12·9	41·0
Salvation Army	7	0·5	4	0·7	—
Other religion (incl. Unitarian)	20	1·6	3	0·5	—
Atheist, agnostic, etc.	48	3·7	4	0·7	7·7
Not stated	8	0·6	11	1·8	—
	1,295	100·0	597	100·0	31·6

Many of the minors could not formally have been *members* of their churches, but clearly this did not deter heads of household from stating their religious affiliation. Only 2·5% of the minors had no definite religious affiliation, compared with 4·3% of adults. Apart from the expected low proportion of atheistic/agnostic minors, the main point that emerges is the (equally expected) difference between the Catholic proportion of all adults and all minors. This is significant at the 1% level; it is consistent with data from other sources and reflects the fairly steep rise in the Catholic 'share' of total live births during the last sixty years.[2]

The religious distribution of the adults in Bishop's Stortford is compared in Table 3 with the summed results of five Gallup Poll quota samples in 1964.[3] The 16–20's have been removed from the Gallup Poll figures, so that both sets of data refer to persons age 21 and over.

Table 3 RELIGIOUS AFFILIATION OF ADULTS
IN BISHOP'S STORTFORD AND GALLUP POLL
DATA: PERCENTAGES

	SRRS data	GALLUP POLL data		
	Bishop's Stortford	London & S.E. Region	England	Great Britain
Church of England	74·5	70·0	69·9	62·5
Nonconformist	9·8	6·9	9·6	10·2
Presbyterian/Church of Scotland	0·7	1·1	1·0	6·9
Roman Catholic	8·6	9·3	9·2	10·0
Other religions	2·1	5·9	3·8	4·1
No religion	3·7	6·8	6·5	6·3
Not stated	0·6	—	—	—
	100·0	100·0	100·0	100·0
N =	1,295	1,177	4,375	5,114

It will be seen that Bishop's Stortford comes closer to the pattern
of religious affiliation for England as a whole than to that for the
London and South-eastern Region. Compared with the latter it has
more Anglicans and Nonconformists, mainly at the expense of the
'other religions', atheists and agnostics.

Table 4 RELIGIOUS AFFILIATION OF MINORS
BORN 1946–1966, BY QUINQUENNIUM OF BIRTH

	1947–51		1952–56		1957–61		1962–66	
	No.	%	No.	%	No.	%	No.	%
Anglican	67	74·4	93	73·8	125	70·6	149	78·0
Nonconformist	17	18·9	8	6·3	15	8·5	14	7·3
Roman Catholic	5	5·6	21	16·7	29	16·4	20	10·5
Other, none, not stated, etc.	1	1·1	4	3·2	8	4·5	8	4·2
	90	100·0	126	100·0	177	100·0	191	100·0

The sharp drop in the Nonconformist figures after the quinquennium
of birth 1947–51 is significant at the 1% level. The sharp rise in the
Catholic figures between 1947–51 and 1952–61 is not quite significant
at the 1% level. The subsequent fall in the Catholic figures does not
reach significance at the 5% level.

COMPOSITION OF HOUSEHOLDS

The size and composition of the 619 households is summarized in Table 5.

Table 5 SIZE AND COMPOSITION OF HOUSEHOLDS

Composition	Total number of persons in household						Total
	1	2	3	4	5	6 and over	
1 adult only	81	—	—	—	—	—	81
1 adult, and minors	—	1	3	2	—	1	7
2 adults only	—	177	—	—	—	—	177
2 adults, and minors	—	—	73	109	49	21	252
3 adults only	—	—	50	—	—	—	50
3 adults, and minors	—	—	—	11	3	5	19
4 or more adults	—	—	—	16	5	1	22
4 or more adults, and minors	—	—	—	—	7	4	11
Total	81	178	126	138	64	32	619

Size of household by religion of household head is given in Table 6:

Table 6 DISTRIBUTION OF HOUSEHOLDS BY SIZE OF HOUSEHOLD AND RELIGION OF HOUSEHOLD HEAD

Religion of household head	Total number of persons in household						Total households	%	Mean size of household
	1	2	3	4	5	6 and over			
Anglican	50	136	97	105	47	19	454	73·2	3·1
Baptist	3	6	6	2	1	—	18	2·9	2·6
Congregationalist	3	6	4	7	2	—	22	3·6	2·9
Methodist	2	6	4	4	4	—	20	3·2	3·1
Presbyterian	—	—	—	2	1	1	4	0·6	4·7
Roman Catholic	7	9	9	9	7	8	49	7·9	3·6
Other and not stated	9	2	3	5	1	3	23	4·4	2·8
Atheist, agnostic, etc.	7	13	3	4	1	1	29	4·9	2·4
Total	81	178	126	138	64	32	619	100·0	3·1
%	13·1	28·7	20·4	22·3	10·3	5·2	100·0		

Some interesting points emerge from this table. The mean size of households with Baptist heads, 2·6, is lower than the sample mean of 3·1, matching the low proportion of Baptist minors. But this is not statistically significant.

The mean size of households with a Catholic head is 3·6, again matching the much higher proportion of Catholic minors. This difference is statistically significant at the 5% level. Catholics headed 15 out of the 96 households having five or more members, i.e. 15·6%. This is significantly different at the 1% level.

Of the 29 atheistic/agnostic heads of household, 20 headed one- or two-person households, and their mean household size was only 2·4. This is not quite significant at the 5% level.

Table 7 relates household size to the religion of the wife of the head of the household.

Table 7   DISTRIBUTION OF HOUSEHOLD, BY SIZE OF HOUSEHOLD, AND RELIGION OF WIFE OF HEAD

Religion of wife of head	Total number of persons in household					Total house-holds	%	Mean size of house-hold
	2	3	4	5	6 and over			
Anglican	120	88	101	48	19	376	76·8	3·4
Baptist	8	6	5	1	—	20	4·1	2·9
Congregationalist	4	3	7	3	—	17	3·5	3·5
Methodist	5	6	4	1	—	16	3·3	3·1
Presbyterian	1	1	1	—	1	4	0·8	3·7
Roman Catholic	5	6	11	7	7	36	7·3	4·2
Other and not stated	1	1	3	2	1	8	1·6	4·0
Atheist, agnostic, etc.	10	2	—	—	1	13	2·6	2·5
Total	154	113	132	62	29	490	100·0	3·4

In the above table (which, of course, excludes one-person households, and those with a female head or a wifeless head), the same three points emerge. The Baptist wives are found in relatively small households (but the difference is not significant), the Roman Catholic wives in relatively large ones (significant at the 1% level), and almost all the atheist/agnostic wives in very small ones. The association between professed atheism, agnosticism etc., and household size can be clearly seen in Table 8.

Table 8 DOMESTIC SITUATION OF ADULT ATHEISTS, AGNOSTICS, HUMANISTS AND RATIONALISTS

	Atheists, agnostics, etc.		Total sample	
	No.	%	No.	%
Living alone	7	14·6	81	6·2
Living in two-person households:				
Head	13	27·1	178	13·7
Wife of head	10	20·8	154	11·9
Other situations	18	37·5	882	68·2
	48	100·0	1,295	1,000·0

Altogether, 62·5% of the atheists, etc., lived in one- or two-person households, compared with only 31·8% in the sample as a whole. The difference is very highly significant at the 1% level.[4]

INTER-FAITH MARRIAGE

Table 9 shows the relationship between religion of head of household and religion of wife. It excludes heads of one-person households, women heads of households and wifeless heads.

Table 9 DISTRIBUTION OF SAMPLE HOUSEHOLDS BY RELIGION OF HOUSEHOLD HEAD AND OF WIFE

	Religion of head of household															
	Anglican		Baptist		Congr.		Methodist		Presbyterian		Catholic		Other, etc.		Atheistic		Total
Religion of wife	No.	%	No.	%	No.	%	No.	%	No.	%	No.	%	No.	%	No.	%	
Anglican	346	93·2	1	6·7	4	25·0	3	17·6	1	25·0	9	25·8	6	60·0	6	30·0	376
Baptist	4	1·1	14	93·3	—		2	11·8	—		—		—		—		20
Congregationalist	5	1·3	—		12	75·0	—		—		—		—		—		17
Methodist	3	0·8	—		—		12	70·6	—		—		—		1	5·0	16
Presbyterian	2	0·5	—		—		—		1	25·0	—		—		1	5·0	4
Roman Catholic	8	2·1	—		—		—		2	50·0	25	71·3	—		1	5·0	36
Other and not stated	2	0·5	—		—		—		—		1	2·9	4	40·0	—		7
Atheist, agnostic, etc	2	0·5	—		—		—		—		—		—		11	55·0	13
Total	372		15		16		17		4		35		10		20		489

Table 10 PROBABILITY OF HUSBANDS &
WIVES IN SAMPLE HAVING A SPOUSE OF
SAME AND DIFFERENT RELIGION IF
RELIGION HAD NO ASSOCIATION WITH
CHOICE OF MARRIAGE PARTNER

Religion of wife	Religion of husband			Religion of husband	Religion of wife		
	Same	Different	Total		Same	Different	Total
Anglican	280·00	96·00	376	Anglican	277·00	95·00	372
Baptist	0·64	19·36	20	Baptist	0·48	14·52	15
Congregationalist	0·60	16·40	17	Congregationalist	0·56	15·44	16
Methodist	0·50	15·50	16	Methodist	0·53	16·47	17
Presbyterian	0·03	3·97	4	Presbyterian	0·03	3·97	4
Roman Catholic	3·06	32·94	36	Roman Catholic	3·01	31·99	35
Other, etc.	0·11	6·89	7	Other, etc.	0·16	9·84	10
Atheist, agnostic, etc.	0·48	12·52	13	Atheist, agnostic, etc.	0·74	19·26	20
Total	285·00	203·58	489	Total	282·51	206·48	489

Table 11 ACTUAL AND EXPECTED NUMBER
OF SPOUSES OF DIFFERENT FAITH

	Actual numbers			Spouses of different faith			
	Husbands	Wives	Total	Expected No.	Actual No.	Actual as % of expected	Index of selectivity
Anglican	372	376	748	191·0	56·0	28·8	71·2
Baptist	15	20	35	33·9	7·0	20·6	79·4
Congregational	16	17	33	31·8	9·0	28·3	71·7
Methodist	17	16	33	32·0	9·0	28·1	71·9
Presbyterian	4	4	8	7·9	6·0	—	—
Roman Catholic	35	36	71	64·9	21·0	32·4	67·6
Other, not stated, etc.	10	7	17	16·7	9·0	—	—
Atheist, agnostic, etc.	20	13	33	31·8	11·0	34·5	65·5
Total	489	489	978	410·0	128·0	31·2	68·8

Table 9 shows that in only 13·1% of households are husband and
wife of different faith: 64 out of 489. Table 10 indicates how many
husbands and how many wives would have a spouse of the same

and how many of a different religion if religion had no association with choice of marriage partner, i.e. if marriage partner had been chosen at random from among the population of Bishop's Stortford. We see that 41·8% of the wives (203·58 out of 489) would have chosen a husband of a different faith, and 42·3% (206·49 out of 489) of the husbands would have chosen a wife of a different faith. These calculations are combined in Table 11 in order to compare the selectivity of the different faiths. Of the 978 husbands and wives, 410 would have a spouse of different faith *if choice were unaffected by religion*, i.e. 42·0%. In fact the actual number who had a spouse of a different faith was only 128, 31·2% of the expected number. This is very highly significant at the 1% level.[5] By calculating the reciprocals we get, in the final column, indices of selectivity. (Figures are not given in the last two columns where the expected number is less than 25.)

Some interesting conclusions emerge from Table 11. Avoidance of inter-faith marriage is pretty general. In almost seven cases out of ten where probability would indicate an inter-faith marriage, it is in fact avoided. This avoidance can reflect social pressures which steer young people away from those of different faiths, or cultural factors which reduce the chance of their meeting those of different faiths, internalized values which predispose them to endogamy, or social and cultural factors causing one party or the other to change his or her religious affiliation before or after the marriage.[6]

The second point that emerges is that there are no marked differences between the different denominations in their *de facto* avoidance of inter-faith marriage. It appears that atheists and agnostics avoid such marriage less emphatically than Christians, and that among Christians avoidance is greatest among Baptists and least among Roman Catholics. But these apparent differences are not statistically significant.

Inter-faith marriages and religion of minors

The total of 619 households included 215 without minors and 129 without spouses. In the remaining 275 households, the head of the household and his wife were of the same religion in 226, leaving 49 where there were minors *and* where head and wife were of different faiths. The data relating to these 49 households was analysed to establish whether there was any tendency for the faith of the minors to follow that of the head or of his wife, or of any religion in particular. In 12 households the situation was too complex to be fitted into simple categories, but in the remaining 37 cases a simple analysis was possible. In two of these 37 households one (or more) of the minors had the same religion as the head of the household *and* another one (or more) had the same religion as his wife. In 23 households *all* the minors had the same religion as the wife, and in 12 the same religion as the head of the household. The difference in the influence of head and wife is not quite significant at the 5% level.

Table 12 NUMBER AND PERCENTAGE OF MIXED FAITH HOUSEHOLDS WHERE MINORS HAVE SAME RELIGION AS HOUSEHOLD HEAD AND HIS SPOUSE RESPECTIVELY

Religion of minors	Same as head		Same as spouse		Total	
	No.	%	No.	%	No.	%
Anglicans	5	38½	14	70	19	58
Nonconformists	1½	25	4	57	5½	42
Presbyterians	—	—	—	—	—	—
Roman Catholics	2½	62½	6	100	8½	85
Other	2	28½	—	—	2	22
Atheist, agnostic	2	40	—	—	2	40
	13	35	24	65	37	—

In Table 12 the Baptists, Congregationalists and Methodists have been grouped together as in none of the 37 households was there a head belonging to one of these three denominations with a spouse belonging to one of the other two. The table suggests that among both heads of households and spouses the Roman Catholics have the most influence of the religion of minors in the household, but the figures are too low for significance.

CONCLUSIONS

The information which emerges from this data necessarily lacks the sharp definition expected of research material: it is a by-product, as the census was not designed to produce statistics or research material. There are in consequence certain vaguenesses. We would like to compare family size of women of different religions; all we can do is to look at household size. We would like to study the influence of parental religion on children's religion; all we can do is to relate 'minors' to head of household and his spouse. Nevertheless, some interesting pointers to further research have emerged.

1. Bishop's Stortford atheists and agnostics tend to be isolates or living in two-person households. Is this a general feature of atheists and agnostics in Britain, or is it a freak situation in one small town? If it is a general phenomenon, is it causally related to unbelief, or consequential upon it? Or is it the consequence of a personality structure that disposes people to reject belief in God? Little research has been done into the sociology of unbelief and isolation has not (to the writer's knowledge) previously been identified as a characteristic of unbelievers.[7]

2. Bishop's Stortford adds a little to the growing evidence that Roman Catholics – contrary to the belief of the Royal Commission on the Population – have larger families than their fellow citizens.[8]

3. Bishop's Stortford households show a generally high level of avoidance of interfaith marriages. Is a similar level of avoidance to be found elsewhere in Britain?

4. Although the numbers are very low, the Bishop's Stortford data offers some support for the Catholic folklore that the religious influence of the mother is greater than that of the father in the religious upbringing of children.

NOTES

1. Registrar General's *Annual Estimates of the Population of England & Wales and of Local Authority areas, 1966*, and *Census, 1961, England & Wales: Preliminary Report*.

2. See A. E. C. W. Spencer, 'The Post-War growth in the Catholic child population of England & Wales' in *Catholic Education: A Handbook, 1960/61*, London: Catholic Education Council for England and Wales, 1960, pp. 18–29.

3. Source: Gallup Poll surveys 356–60. Figures quoted by kind permission of Social Surveys (Gallup Poll) Ltd.

4. Chi square $=15.56$, df $=1$.

5. Chi square $=334$, df $=1$.

6. Conversion of either party before or after marriage represents one aspect of such rejection.

7. For an interesting exposition of the sociological approach to unbelief, see Theo. M. Steeman, *The Study of atheism: Sociological approach*, FERES (International Federation of Institutes for Social and Socio-Religious Research), Louvain, 1965, mineographed.

8. See A. E. C. W. Spencer, 'The demography and sociography of the Roman Catholic community of England and Wales', in L. Bright and S. Clements (Ed.), *The Committed Church*, London: Darton, Longman and Todd, 1966, pp. 74–75.

10 Comments on some Gallup Poll Statistics

Bernice Martin

OVER THE last decade information about the religious life of Great Britain has begun to accumulate piecemeal after an astonishing lapse of interest in the whole subject for over fifty years. Even today we are probably less well informed about religious beliefs and the incidence of church-going in our society than were the contemporaries of Horace Mann and Dr Hume after the 1851 religious census. One of the few continuing and largely unused sources of information about British religion in recent years has been the data gathered by opinion poll agencies on the beliefs and attitudes of the churches. What follows is an analysis of material collected for a variety of purposes over the last four years and recently tabulated by Gallup Poll. Miss Leslie Austen of Social Surveys (Gallup Poll) Ltd, to whom grateful thanks are here offered, was responsible for having this data prepared and made available for publication.

Before commenting on the findings of these surveys a few preliminary remarks are necessary. In the first place, though much of what follows is critical comment this should not be understood as reflecting in any way on Gallup Poll. My point is that the random collection of topical material which is perfectly appropriate to an opinion poll agency is not necessarily, indeed perhaps it cannot be, as useful to the sociology of religion as specially designed statistical surveys constructed on the basis of considered hypotheses. It is the lack of the latter rather than the inevitable and tantalizing omissions and ambiguities of the former about which the sociologist may legitimately complain. Nevertheless, it is necessary to point not only to the instructive and suggestive findings of these opinion polls but also to the limitations in their usefulness to the sociology of religion. And one may appropriately begin with the caveats.

Firstly, some of the surveys reveal little to us now because of elements of ambiguity or topicality in the phrasing of the question.

A simple answer may cloak nuances of interpretation and a variety of attitudes motivations and identifications a knowledge of which alone could make sense of the resulting percentages. The questions on the Rhodesia crisis show this limitation most clearly but there are others which will be noted in the detailed discussion. Secondly, it is a pity that the categories of religious bodies have been changed from time to time. In most of the surveys quoted here the categories were Church of England (C. of E.), Nonconformist (N.C.), Church of Scotland (C. of S.), Roman Catholic (R.C.) and 'the rest' or 'others'. In one case, however, this became C. of E., C. of S., Free Church, R.C., 'other' and 'none', and in a further case, in which presumably the focus of attention was a comparision between Anglican and Catholic opinions it became C. of E., R.C., 'other' and 'none'. The inclusion of 'none' is intriguing and instructive as will be seen below, but to link N.C., C. of S., Orthodox, Pentecostals, Jews, Muslims, Hindus, etc., together as 'other' produces what for the present purpose is meaningless heterogeneity rather than a usable category. There is in addition a slight danger that in all the surveys the small sects – Witnesses, Brethren, Christadelphians, etc. – may have been split between Nonconformity and the 'other religion' category. Their actual numbers must have been very small but the confusion is regrettable.

Analysis of response by social class is hampered by the very broad class categories. Usually the main division is occupational, producing manual and non-manual groups, but in one case the categories appear to be predominantly income-based, Average +, Average, Average −, and Very Poor.

The age categories are equally unsophisticated. They are very wide – 15 or 20 years – and may obscure the effects of relevant turning points in religious and social behaviour for this reason. For instance the 16 to 29 age group stretches from near-maximum adolescent belief and practice well into the fallow period associated with family building and early child rearing; or again the 45 to 64 age group extends for a man from the most active part of his career to retirement or for a woman either from the peak of domestic responsibilities to virtual redundancy or alternatively the whole span of her main post-maternal paid employment. It will be seen from the detailed analyses below that narrower age categories would often be more useful and appropriate.

Finally and most seriously, the value of the results for the sociology of religion is impaired by the size of the samples. Although 1,000 to 1,500 is normally considered an 'adequate' sample size, adequacy must depend on the number and type of cross classifications and correlations to which the data needs to be subjected if it is to yield crucial information. Although the findings of the surveys as they stand can give a gross impression of the views of the major religious groups in Britain, this impression may on closer scrutiny prove to be misleading because it is not possible to discover from the data presented here the importance of the religious factor *per se*. To get anywhere near this objective through a statistical study one would need to compare the responses of the different churches with at least age, sex and social class held constant, and perhaps in addition one might need to take into account the different regional concentrations of the churches. (The one case in which opinion on abortion is classified by region suggests that local traditions may have their effects as well as different age and class concentrations.) None of this can usefully be done with the present figures because the numbers in most of the church sub-samples are too small: apart from the C. of E. none of the churches has many more than 100 respondents in any of these surveys. To take an extreme but by no means irrelevant case it is clear that one would find no more than a handful of practising R.C. professionally employed women, yet one might well need to isolate such a group if one were trying to estimate the relative importance of social class, sex, employment experience and educational attainment in relation to religious belief and its translation into social and political terms. The fact that the present samples have not been and because of their size cannot usefully be broken down in this way means that one needs constantly to take subjective and therefore inaccurate account of the different age, sex and class composition of the churches. One cannot know how different a comparison of, say, N.C. and R.C. opinions would be if one could accurately allow for the youth and relatively lower social status of the R.C.s and the greater age and probably slightly higher status of the Nonconformists. Or again, what is one to make of the surprisingly illiberal views of those professing no religion? They are clearly not all Brigid Brophys and Freddy Ayers. Does this indicate that the lowest status groups of all are such thorough non-joiners that they do not even claim residual church allegiance, or could it be that middle-class Humanists (supposing always that Humanism has not slipped into the 'other religions' category) are more reactionary on abortion and ethnic minorities than the *New Statesman* has led us to expect?

The special study of 400 Roman Catholics (see Table 14) shows something of what needs to be done if one is to make reliable comparisons of the churches' positions. The distinction between adherents who go to church often and those who go rarely or not at all is clearly very important and one which American studies of church practice have employed for some time. But even the survey of Catholics is less telling than it might be because this valuable distinction is only used in one dimension. There is no breakdown by social class, age and sex for the two categories *separately*, the regular and the irregular or non-attenders. The figures do not tell us, for example, whether the upper status groups are more likely than lower status groups to go to Mass regularly. They can give no more than tantalizing indications of whether the factor of class, age, sex or regularity of practice is most clearly related to a desire for 'liberalizing' and ecumenical change in the Roman Church. While it appears crudely that those who practise rarely are more in favour of such changes than the regular church-goers there are also indications of greater flexibility and liberality of opinions among higher status groups. If, as one suspects, the practising are on average of higher social status than the residual adherents, then one is faced with an interesting paradox which might, for instance, mean that the connection between social status and liberal opinions works in opposite directions for the practising and non- or hardly-practising groups, or alternatively that the high status/liberality connection holds for both groups but is less dominant than the high practice/orthodoxy connection. Without a further cross-classification of this or some future sample one cannot know.

To include the practising and the dormant adherents together in an analysis of the churches' opinions may distort the picture more for some churches than others. It is more than probable that the dormant form a higher proportion of C. of E. respondents than for other churches. It seems likely that since the 1851 Census, when the C. of E. and Nonconformity were neck-and-neck, there has been a gradual drift of the non- or rarely-practising from residual Free Church allegiance towards the national church. The likelihood of there being an unusually heavy weighting of barely-practising adherents among the C. of E. respondents makes it particularly important to discover whether, as among the Roman Catholics, this dormant group holds markedly more radical and non-authoritatian views than do the regular church-goers. If this were so the striking liberality of Anglicans on most of the issues raised in these surveys might prove partly illusory. Without further research one can only speculate.

The following analysis then should not be regarded as a definitive delineation of the opinions of the British churches on the issues in question. It could more fruitfully be seen as an outline of some problems and paradoxes which future empirical research in this field might investigate.

With these reservations let us examine the surveys.

Some Gallup Poll Surveys 1963–67

The first point of substance which arises is that the nine random samples ranging from 926 to 1501 respondents, produce figures of church adherence (i.e. regular and irregular practice together) which confirm the figures currently available.[1] The C. of E. varies between almost 57% and almost 64%; Nonconformity between almost 9% and over 12%; Roman Catholicism between 10% and almost 13%; the Church of Scotland (which because of its regional concentration is most liable to varied representation) between 4% and 9·5% with 7% the most frequent and probably the most reliable figure; and 'the rest' between 11% and 16%, with 11% the most frequent figure. In the two cases where 'the rest' are meaningfully divided into 'other religions' and 'none', one sees respectively 6% and between 4% and 8% in these two categories.

The Durkheimian dominance of the C. of E. is therefore clearly demonstrated, however tenuous the links may be for many who claim identification with the national church. The rough numerical equivalence of Roman Catholic and Nonconformists numbers is also confirmed. The population balance here is probably tipping fairly rapidly in favour of the Roman Catholics who are younger and more prolific as a group than Nonconformists. The latter are suffering from the continued demographic effects of a lower than average birth rate during most of this century and may expec ta further proportionate decline over the next few decades. Other religions will probably continue to experience a slow increase in absolute numbers and in proportion due to the influx of non-Christian and Eastern Orthodox immigrants with relatively high birth rates, and to the success of the many small Christian and pseudo-Christian sects and cults among the relatively deprived and the anomic. The very small proportion of the population disclaiming all religious identification in what is popularly described as 'secular' society has been stressed elsewhere and needs no further comment here.

Since the surveys were carried out *ad hoc* they do not form a planned whole. Nevertheless, it is possible to group the questions raised under four main heads: (1) theological, (2) organizational and ecumenical, (3) social/moral, and (4) political. These will be discussed in turn below. There is a good deal of overlap between categories, and where this is particularly notable it will be referred to in the detailed discussion.

I   Theological Questions

These questions are concerned with belief in God, Christ, the Devil and life after death. All four occurred in the same survey conducted by Gallup Poll in spring 1963.

Clearly the main focus of interest here is the degree of 'orthodoxy' which each church displayed, but as the outset one needs to note the crudity of the index. Too often in American studies one has found orthodoxy equated with literalism or fundamentalism in such a way that the most subtle of the early Christian fathers and the English sixteenth-century divines would have found themselves outside the pale. We do not know what nuances of interpretation the respondents here placed upon the particular set of opinions from which they had to choose. A belief in 'some sort of spirit/god or life force' may represent vague, residual theism or a well thought-out metaphysical position well within the main stream of Christian theology. Particularly since it is the alternative formulation to belief in a 'personal god', respondents may well have seen it as the 'code' for a liberal as against the conservative-evangelical or fundamentalist group identification. It is perhaps also misleading to offer alternative formulations of the godhead but not of the devil – why not ask whether there is some sort of spirit/devil or force of evil? Without this choice we cannot safely assume that belief in the devil is directly analogous to both categories of belief in God taken together.

With considerable reservations then about the real meaning of surface 'orthodoxy', each question will be taken in turn.

(1) *Belief in God* (see Table 1a)

   38% of the respondents believed in a 'personal god';
   33% believed in 'some sort of spirit/god or life force';

20% 'did not know what to think';
9% did not believe in 'any sort of spirit/god or life force'.

The figure of 71% for belief in a god (however defined) though still a large majority belief, is lower than in some previous opinion polls where figures of 85% have been found.[2] On the basis of this one sample it would be premature to suggest a decline in this belief. The shift, if it is in fact occurring, appears to be to a 'don't know' response (20%) rather than to atheism (9% in this sample). It might be as well to note here that 'don't know' can as easily represent confusion or vacillation between the alternative definitions of God as an inability to opt for belief or disbelief. It would be unwise to assume that a 'don't know' response is the same as intellectual agnosticism, that is, the contention that man *cannot* know. Both disbelief and 'don't know' responses were, predictably, higher among 'the rest' (which here includes 'No religion') than in any of the churches, but even so 52% of 'the rest' believed in some sort of god. It is perhaps even more notable, however, that of all the churches only the R.C. had no disbelievers. One would like to know how these atheistic adherents distribute themselves between the practising and non-practising segments of their churches, and how they cope with the apparent dissonance between intellectual position and institutional identification. In both the C. of E. and N.C. a slightly higher proportion opted for 'life force' than for the 'personal god' formulation, and as many as 22% in the C. of E. and 18% in Nonconformity did not know what to think. The similarity of the C. of E. and N.C. response is parallelled by the perhaps more surprising closeness of the R.C. and C. of S. figures. The latter pair, at the two opposite ends of the Catholic/Protestant spectrum were notably more 'orthodox' than the former.

The relation between social class and belief in a god is fairly clear. There is a 10% increase in belief among the non-manual as against the manual categories. Moreover the manual groups produce more 'don't know' answers and more disbelief than do the non-manual groups, all of which confirms one's expectations from similar studies here and in other societies. Of the believers the manual other (i.e. unskilled and semi-skilled) group and the professional/managerial group are both slightly more inclined to believe in a personal god than in a life force while in the remaining two (skilled manual and 'non-manual other') are fairly evenly divided between the two formulations. The sex difference runs in the expected direction with women believing more and choosing the 'personal god' formulation more often, and disbelieving, or having no firm opinion, less often than men.

The analysis by age categories is intriguing and not quite the simple increase of belief and orthodoxy with advancing years which one has come to expect. The high point for belief, taking the two formulations of the godhead together, is the 45 to 64 age group, while the highest belief in a 'personal god', but by far the lowest belief in a 'life force' comes in the 65+ group. Consequently one would find a curve for belief in a god (both formulations) which rises smoothly to the 45 to 64 age group and drops a sharp 8% in the 65+ group, and a similar shaped curve with an even sharper dip at 65+ for belief in a 'life force', while belief in a personal god increases steadily with each increase in age. It is perhaps worth noting also that, while belief in a personal god is stronger than belief in a life force in all age groups, the gap is only large in the 65+ group.

The 'don't know' response is the obverse of the belief response. Its lowest point is the 45–64 age group, with a noticeable increase in the 65+ group. Disbelief in God is correspondingly at its lowest among the 45 to 64 group and then shows a slight increase at 65+ though not to the level of the two youngest groups.

The figures for the 65+ group are very puzzling. Of all age groups this must be the most predominantly female. This may partly explain the big difference between the two types of belief in God among the oldest group since belief in a personal god is characteristic of women, but other puzzles like the increase of disbelief remain. The figures do not suggest a simple increase of 'belief' with increasing age. Amongst the oldest group it is the 'orthodox', 'literalist', 'anthropomorphic' or 'old-fashioned' formulation (depending on one's point of view) which has strongest support and which may be no more than a simple reflection of the theological climate in the formative years of the generation concerned. If this finding is due to anything more than sampling error it is worth further investigation. It is not possible to see from these figures whether greater uncertainty and a decline in belief in a 'life force' sets in somewhere within the 45–64 age group or indeed whether with smaller age categories a regular curve would be revealed at all. It seems particularly important to sub-divide the 45–64 age group since it is both the largest category and the most heterogeneous in terms of life patterns.

(2) *Belief in Christ* (see Table 1b)

59% of the respondents believed that Christ was the Son of God;
17% believed that he was just a man;
8% thought he was just a story;
16% did not know what to think.

As in the previous question, the C. of E. and N.C. have almost identical responses, while the R.C.s are more strictly orthodox. Both the C. of E. and N.C. have substantial minorities who do not believe the divinity of Christ (20% and 21% respectively) and the C. of S., while producing a higher percentage of believers, has roughly the same proportion of unbelievers (22%) as the C. of E. and N.C. While the C. of S. and the R.C. may be close together on theism, on the status of Christ the Calvinists show more affinities with their Protestant neighbours. As with belief in God, the 'don't knows' are almost as prominent in the C. of E. as among 'the rest'. The one R.C. who believed Christ was just a story might have been a fascinating case study.

The findings for age, sex and social class are in no way unexpected. There is a slight but clear increase of orthodox belief and a decrease of the 'don't know' response with higher social class and with increasing age. The latter makes the odd age curve for belief in God the more puzzling. Women again are considerably more orthodox than men and less likely to return 'don't know' answers.

(3) *Life after Death* (See Table 1c)

53% of the respondents believed there was a life after death;
22% did not believe this;
25% did not know what to believe.

As in some other surveys on this point one finds belief in immortality on the one hand and disbelief or no firm opinion on the other, roughly evenly divided in the population: 53% to 47% here. 'The rest' score higher on disbelief and lower on belief than any of the churches. C. of E. and Nonconformist figures are again very similar, though there are slightly more 'don't know' responses and less disbelief in N.C. than in the C. of E. R.C. and C. of S. results are also close and both notably more 'orthodox' than the previous pair. Non-manual groups show greater belief than manual groups and women are more orthodox than men, as one expects. But belief in immortality, like belief in a god, has a curious age distribution. Belief rises with each age step up to the 45–64 age group but drops 5% in the 65+ group. Again, the question must be raised as to whether increases in Christian belief are part of the process of ageing in our culture, or whether perhaps we are measuring the effects of the socialization, formal teaching and early experiences of particular generations, effects which do not change much through the life cycle of the generation concerned but simply appear in successively older age categories over time. To put the problem crudely, do the over-65s show this decline in belief in immortality because the nearer they approach to death the more stoically realistic they become? (If the figures showed a steady rise one could, of course, argue much more persuasively that the nearer death the greater is the need for reassurance!) Or is it perhaps that this generation, whose youth was dominated by the first World War, suffered losses of faith as well as life in that formative period? Again the present data is not of a kind which can resolve this problem. This odd statistic again points to the need for a planned study of religious belief and age.

(4) *Belief in the Devil* (See Table 1d)

36% of the respondents believed in the devil;
46% did not believe in the devil;
18% did not know what to think.

This is the only one of the four theological questions on which disbelief is greater than belief. The R.C.s here, as in the previous questions, are the most strictly 'orthodox' of the churches, though even this group included 29% of unbelievers on this issue. The C. of S. is the next most 'orthodox' group having, like the Catholics, a clear majority of believers. The C. of E. and N.C. both show more disbelief than belief (though in N.C. the gap is a mere 1%) and both have substantial minorities who returned 'don't know' answers. As in previous questions, though the C. of E. and N.C. pattern is close there is more disbelief in the former and a larger 'don't know' section in the latter. 'The rest', as expected, disbelieve more and believe less than any of the churches. Belief is again stronger in the non-manual than in the manual class and among women than men, though the differences in both cases are slight.

For the third time the age curve displays some curiosities. The maximum belief and minimum disbelief both occur at 65+ while minimum belief and maximum disbelief are found at 30–44 with the 16–29 and the 45–64 age groups almost identical in their response. Disbelief is stronger than belief at all ages, and perhaps the most important observation here is that the differences between age groups on this issue are very slight indeed.

To summarize: it was found for these four theological propositions in descending order of popularity that:

(1) 71% of the sample had some kind of belief in a god while 9% rejected all belief;
(2) Christ was held to be the Son of God by 59% while his divinity was rejected in various ways by 25%;
(3) 53% believed in life after death and 22% disbelieved;
(4) 39% believed and 46% disbelieved in a devil.

Of the major British churches the R.C.s were the most 'orthodox', followed closely by the C. of S., with N.C. and C. of E. producing similar and less orthodox patterns of response. There was consistently greater orthodoxy in the non-manual than in the manual classes and among women than men. The relation between belief and age was neither entirely consistent nor easily explicable.

II Questions on Ecumenism and Church Organization

There are three sources of data under this heading; two surveys undertaken in September and October 1962 and in January 1967 in which questions on ecumenical negotiations between churches were included, and, thirdly, substantial sections of the special survey of Roman Catholics, especially questions 5, 6 and 12 which concern the relations of the Catholic Church and other Christian bodies.

(1) *September and October 1962: Negotiations between all Christian Churches* (see Table 2)
(a) 60% of respondents said they would approve if there were negotiations between all the churches – R.C., Greek Orthodox, C. of E. and all the other churches in the world – on the question of their uniting;
25% said they would disapprove;
15% did not know what to think.

By a small margin the Free Churches were the most enthusiastic, having the highest approval and lowest disapproval figures. The C. of E. was only slightly less approving and more disapproving, followed very closely by the R.C. church with the same approving but a higher disapproving proportion. The C. of S. had a considerably lower approval figure and a disapproving proportion which though a minority was almost twice the Free Church figure. The 'other religions' group and even more clearly the 'no religion' group were less favourable to such negotiations than any of the churches though indifference was more characteristic of the non-religious, and disapproval of the 'other religion' group. The latter would of course include not only non-Christians but sectarians who would refuse to consider being yoked with the ungodly in ecumenical union.

Unexpectedly men and women scored identical approval scores, though men disapproved more than women. There was no analysis by age or social class.

(*b*) 26% of respondents thought that such negotiations were likely to be successful;

57% thought that they were not likely to be successful;

17% did not know what to think.

There was strikingly little variation of opinion between the churches on the likely success of such negotiations and the only clear feature of these figures is the larger 'don't know' category among those of 'other' and 'no religion' as compared with the churches. The only conclusion that one can reasonably draw from this survey is that to approve of ecumenical negotiations is by no means the same thing as expecting them to succeed. One wonders what the different churches saw as the major obstacles to unity, and one suspects that since all were more willing to participate than they were optimistic of the result, they may well have seen other people's intransigence rather than their own as likely to frustrate the enterprise.

(2) *January 1967: Negotiations between C. of E. and N.C.* (see Table 3a)

59% of respondents said they would approve if there were negotiations between the C. of E. and N.C. churches on the question of their uniting.

14% said they would disapprove;

18% said that they would not mind;

9% said that they did not know what to think.

Approval for these bilateral negotiations was roughly the same as that for the wider ecumenical negotiations mooted in the earlier survey with an additional 18% who would not mind, while disapproval was 11% less. The highest rate of approval and least disapproval came from the C. of E. More surprising on the face of it is the marginally greater enthusiasm of R.C.s than N.C.s, particularly in view of the 1962 survey findings. The lowest approval, the lowest 'don't mind' figure and the only significant disapproval (32%) among the churches came from the C. of S. 'The rest' were even less approving but indifference rather than disapproval accounts for this.

One might venture to explain the divergence between this and the findings of the 1962 survey by noting the different implications of the phrasing of the questions in the two surveys. The earlier survey clearly put all participants in the negotiations on the same footing – the specific mention of the Greek Orthodox Church served to reinforce the international reference and guard against a purely British interpretation of the doctrinal and status issues which ecumenism might locally involve. In the later survey the reference would immediately be understood as British by most respondents. It is perhaps relevant too that the possibility of negotiations between Anglicans and Methodists had recently been explored by the two churches so that this question alone of the three in this section would be seen as referring to a likely rather than a remote prospect.

The high Free Church approval of negotiations between all Christian churches which the 1962 survey revealed was probably a reflection of the liberal and democratic ethos of Dissent which predominates unless fears are raised that ecumenism may mean catholicization and curtailment of independence. One strongly suspects that behind the findings of the 1967 survey is a feeling that unity between Anglican and Nonconformist churches, the latter having split off from the former, would involve the offspring's adopting more elements of the parent church's pattern than the parent would take from the offspring: or put another way that unity would mean symbolic if not doctrinal movement in a Catholic rather than a Protestant direction.

The presence of a large Calvinist element in the theology and organization of the C. of S., together with its role as a focus for Scottish national identity, are probably sufficient to explain the mistrust which this church feels about all ecumenical moves.

More women than men approved of negotiations between the C.

of E. and N.C. churches, and men were found to disapprove slightly
more often. Since men appear to be less involved in religious belief
and practice than women their higher disapproval figure is interesting and a little surprising. Is this masculine intolerance or one of the
very few issues over which men are more conservative than women?
A mere 2% difference may, of course, be statistically insignificant.

The figures for approval by age groups followed a similar pattern of
increase with higher involvement in religion (so far, that is, as the
results of the theological questions can indicate). There was an increase of approval with each age step up to the 45–64 group and then
a decline at 65+. It is perhaps worth noting that this is a different
sample from the one used to sound out theological beliefs, so that
the fact of finding this same curious age curve strengthens the suspicion that a sampling error cannot entirely explain the unexpected
reactions of the 65+ age group. Again one might note that since
women are more in favour of ecumenical negotiations than men it is
surprising to find a decline in approval in a group where women must
predominate.

There was on average more approval and less disapproval amongst
non-manual than amongst manual workers – again suggesting approval alongside belief. But perhaps more significant and apparently con-
tradicting the previous point is the fact that the lowest approval and
highest disapproval figure come from the skilled manual group, the
only section of the working classes likely to contain substantial
numbers of regular church-goers.

January 1967: Negotiations between R.C. and other churches (see
   Table 3b)
   48% of respondents said that they would approve if there were
      negotiations between the R.C. church and all other churches in
      this country on the question of their uniting;
   26% said they would not approve;
   15% said that they would not mind;
   10% did not know what to think.

The findings on this question were very much what the results of
the previous one would lead one to expect, with rates of approval
descending regularly from the Catholic to the Protestant end of the
spectrum. Roman Catholics had the highest rate of approval, which
at 62% was 3% higher than their approval of Anglican/N.C. nego-

tiations. They also showed the lowest rate of disapproval among the churches, though it is important to note that for Catholics as well as the other major churches, there was considerably greater disapproval of negotiations between the R.C. and other churches than of C. of E./N.C. negotiations: more is probably felt to be at stake when the Catholics are indicated as host in negotiations on unity. The C. of E. approval was 12% less than its approval of negotiations with N.C. churches and its disapproval figure was 13% higher. This may reflect a sense of being at a disadvantage should the structure of the negotiations place the English national church on the same footing in relation to the Catholic hierarchy as all other 'separated brethren'; but it could equally indicate that fellow-feeling for Protestants is stronger than Catholic sympathies in the Anglican church.

Nonconformist disapproval was more than twice that in the previous question while the C. of S.'s disapproval exceeded its approval figure (though approval together with 'don't mind' responses still slightly exceeded disapproval). 'The rest' had lower approval but also a considerably smaller disapproval figure than any of the churches. The impression strongly remains that non-Catholics felt that the phrasing of the question suggested negotiations about *reunion with Rome* and not as did the phrasing of the question in the 1962 survey, an entirely democratic discussion in which all participants would start from equivalent status and strength.

Women again approved more often than men though by contrast with (*a*) they also disapproved more. Again the difference was a mere 2%. Men returned more 'don't know' and 'don't mind' answers, probably because of a lower sense of involvement in the issue.

There was greater approval among the non-manual than the manual class but disapproval was roughly equal in the two groups. Again, however, one should note that the highest disapproval came from the skilled manual workers.

The findings for age are once more puzzling but may well be explicable in this case by the different age composition of the churches – N.C. numbers being weighted towards older groups and R.C. numbers towards younger ones. Maximum approval came at 30–44, while minimum approval, minimum 'don't mind' responses and by far the greatest disapproval came at 65+.

The findings of the two previous surveys can be supplemented by the special survey of Roman Catholics (Table 14), where similar but not identical questions were asked about relations between the

Roman Catholic and other churches. The most nearly parallel
questions were 5 and 6. In answer to question 5, 81% of the 400
Catholics said that they thought the relations of the R.C. and other
Christian churches in Britain ought to be closer than they are at
present: 13% said they should not be; 7% did not know what to
think. One does not know, of course, in what sense respondents
understood 'closer relations' – as more joint activities, moves towards
reunion on Rome's terms, concessions to Protestantism, etc.

Approval came more from irregular than regular attenders at
Mass and disapproval more from the latter. Women and the upper
social classes were more inclined to approve and less inclined to
disapprove than men and lower social classes.

In answer to question 6, 'Do you think that all Christian denominations should take positive steps to unite in one church or would you
be against such a move?' the pattern of approval and disapproval
was closely similar to that for question 5, but with generally lower
approval and higher disapproval. The R.C.s in the special sample
were less enthusiastic and more disapproving of this suggestion than
were the Catholic respondents in the 1962 survey on ecumenical
negotiations (see Table 2a). Perhaps 'positive steps to unite in one
church' are more alarming than 'negotiations'.

The R.C. survey included several other questions with indirect
ecumenical implications in that they concerned the church's organization and worship, and its relations with non-Catholics. Questions
1 to 4 concern the church's authority over its members and test
opinion on certain changes which might be regarded as moves in
the direction of the Protestant churches – relaxation of authority,
greater lay participation in the running of the church, an end of
compulsory clerical celibacy, liturgical changes such as the replace-
ment of Latin by English in the Mass, a more flexible policy about
mixed marriages and the maintenance of R.C. schools.

The degree to which innovation on these issues was welcomed
varied considerably. Eighty-six per cent thought Cardinal Heenan
was doing a good job, more among regular than irregular church-
goers, but with no sex or class differences. Fifty-three per cent of
respondents accepted the authority of the church without question
– 20% more among regular than among irregular church-goers –
while 40% of regular and 51% of irregular attenders accepted it with
some reservations. Women were more inclined than men, and lower
than upper classes, to accept authority without question. Fifty-

F

seven per cent felt the church's authority over its members was about right (more among regular church-goers and women than their counterparts but with minute class differences) while 36% felt it was too strict (more irregular church-goers and men) and a mere 7% that it was not strict enough (remarkably, more among the lower than the upper classes here). The paradox involved in these figures was commented on in the introductory comments but is worth restating here. It is likely on the basis of other sources that the higher social classes rather than lower classes will be found to attend church regularly, yet here we see acceptance without reservation of the church's authority and even a feeling that this authority should be stricter characterizing the *lower* social classes *and* the regular church-goers. It probably means that the lower-class version of Catholicism is more inflexible than that of the more highly educated and higher status groups, and partly in consequence of its rigidity is, perhaps, more easily undermined.

Fifty per cent, equally divided between regular and irregular attenders, approved the idea of greater lay participation in the affairs of the R.C. church (slightly more among men and upper social classes). The only notable differences in disapproval of this issue were between regular and irregular attenders, the latter disapproving less than the former, conservatism therefore being again marginally stronger in the institutionally involved.

Eighty-two per cent, an overwhelming majority, approved the use of English in the Mass, a change already introduced. Regular and irregular church-goers approved in equal proportions but women (more institutionally involved) were more enthusiastic than men, and the lower (probably less institutionally involved) than the upper social classes. Latin may well be more meaningful to the latter; its abandonment may even be felt to involve loss of status by some.

There was an almost equal division of opinion on clerical celibacy. A bare minority of 40% felt that priests should be either encouraged or permitted to marry (more among the irregular church-goers, men and lower social classes), while 44% supported priestly celibacy.

Sixty-five per cent approved the continuation of R.C. 'elementary' (*sic*) schools (slightly more regular than irregular church-goers but with no important sex or class differences). Fifty-four per cent felt that the present rules about R.C.s marrying non-Catholics should be either abandoned or made easier (more irregular church-goers, men and lower social classes), and 37% felt they should be left as they were (notably more regular than irregular church-goers). The idea of relaxing the rule that all Catholics must bring up their children as Catholics in cases of mixed marriage had less than majority support, only 41% compared with 45% who opposed relaxation. Irregular church-goers, lower social classes, and women, on whom the main burden of religious upbringing within the family usually lies, were more in favour of relaxation.

In general then, though not on every single issue, the suggested changes had more support from the less institutionally involved – the men, the lower social classes and the irregular church-goers – though most of them had very substantial support from all Catholics. The only significantly conservative opinion was on the need to maintain separate Catholic 'elementary' education.

III Social/Moral Questions

(1) The Influence of Religion on British Life

This question fits only uneasily into any category of issues, but perhaps is most nearly appropriate here. It is an imprecise question which might be understood as referring to faith, churchgoing, public morality, the content of TV programmes, religious education in schools, the modesty or immodesty of current fashions, rates of divorce, illegitimacy, crime and a thousand and one other things that might be used as an index of decency and Christianity in Britain.

Two separate surveys included a question on this issue, in May 1965 and May 1967 (see Tables 4a and 4b). In 1965 11% and in 1967 9% of respondents thought that religion as a whole was increasing its influence on British life; in 1965 20% and in 1967 19% thought its influence was about the same; in 1965 55% and in 1967 65% thought its influence was decreasing; in 1965 14% and in 1967 8% did not know what to think.

The most striking feature is the 10% increase over this short period in the proportion who thought the influence of religion was declining. One strongly suspects that this additional 10%, appearing largely at the expense of the 'don't know' category, were simply reacting to a wave of masochistic publicity which the churches, especially the C. of E., gave themselves in this two years. The suspicion is strengthened by the fact that the biggest increase in this category came in the C. of E. – from 55% to 69%. In 1967 the C. of E. figure was higher even than that in the 'No religion' category.

This finding is probably a better measure of the influence of the popular press than of the influence of religion.

(2) *March–April, 1963: Standards of Public Behaviour* (see Table 5)

This question has much in common with the previous one. It is ambiguous and therefore difficult to comment on. 'Standards of public behaviour' is a phrase which will have different resonance depending on the total frame of reference of the respondent and perhaps on topical public scandals, such as the Profumo affair. One may then be measuring opinion on a variety of issues ranging from politeness to violent political protest, or from the vandalism of football crowds to the private sexual mores of public figures. For what the findings are worth they show that:

43% of respondents were satisfied with standards of public behaviour;

46% were dissatisfied;

11% did not know what to think.

The preoccupation with moral questions and the strand of perfectionism which has characterized Puritanism and its offshoots may partly explain why N.C. and C. of S. were the most dissatisfied of the churches, followed by C. of E., which as so often fits the national average, and with R.C.s least dissatisfied. These figures are the slenderest straw on which to hang a theory but at least one can note that they do not contradict Weber's distinction between the ethic of Catholicism and Protestantism.

Class differences were very slight but it may be worth noting that skilled manual workers were somewhat surprisingly most satisfied and least dissatisfied. Here, unlike the findings for theological questions, there was a simple age curve, with satisfaction decreasing and dissatisfaction increasing with each step up the age scale. Men were considerably more satisfied and less dissatisfied than women.

(3) *Abortion*

Three surveys explored the churches' attitudes to abortion, the special survey of R.C.s and two general surveys undertaken in February 1966 and January 1967. Abortion law reform was being seriously debated during the period between the surveys, but the law was not changed until after the later of the two investigations.

The two general samples yielded the following results (see Tables 6 and 7):

(*a*) Where the health of the mother is in danger the respondents regarded legal abortion as follows:

In 1966 79% and in 1967 86% approved;
In 1966 9% and in 1967 7% disapproved;
In 1966 12% and in 1967 7% did not know what to think.

(*b*) Where the child may be born deformed:

In 1966 71% and in 1967 76% approved;
In 1966 13% and in 1967 13% disapproved;
In 1966 16% and in 1967 11% did not know what to think.

(*c*) Where the family does not have enough money to support another child:

In 1966 33% and in 1967 37% approved;
In 1966 43% and in 1967 46% disapproved;
In 1966 24% and in 1967 17% did not know what to think.

Two general points arise from these figures. First, it seems that approval of legal abortion gained some ground over the year between the two surveys and the 'don't know' response decreased, but disapproval remained fairly constant. This must surely be related to the publicity which the issue was given over the period. One is tempted to draw a parallel with studies of voting behaviour where one also finds that public debate, while it may help to make up the mind of the undecided, seldom produces dramatic conversion among those who start with firm opinions. The second general point is that the respondents seem to have regarded the three cases in descending order of sympathy. A large majority approved of legal abortion in cases (*a*) and (*b*) but a minority only in case (*c*). Yet how clear is this opinion? One suspects that the phrase 'When the health of the mother is in danger' was understood in very many different ways ranging from the situation where a choice has to be made between the life of the mother and that of the unborn child, down to the case where the birth of the child may constitute some threat to the peace of mind or the material comfort of the mother and might in consequence be liberally regarded as a danger to her mental health: worry about possible deformity or the financial consequences of an extra child might well be a danger of this kind. Some respondents who committed themselves to approving the general principle of (*a*) (the then operative law) may well have deplored the most liberal cases of its application if the response in cases (*b*) and even more crucially (*c*) is to be trusted. One might note a further ambiguity in the wording of case (*c*) which begs the question of who is to make the judgement on the sufficiency of the family's income and of the standard at which the additional child should be supported.

The response of the churches in each case will now be considered.

(*a*) Legal abortion where the health of the mother is in danger

In 1966 only the C. of E. had a higher rate of approval than the national average, though the Free Churches and then 'other religions' were both fairly close. The C. of S. had an approval figure 10% below the average. The R.C.s predictably and those professing no religion surprisingly both scored the lowest approval – 57% against a general average of 79% – though the latter were less disapproving and more inclined to return 'don't know' answers.

A curious change occurred by January 1967. The C. of S. returned the highest approval rate, a spectacular 95%. This may have been in response to a public pronouncement on the issue by the church's officials. There was no parallel increase in C. of S. approval of legal abortion in cases (*b*) and (*c*). The order of the churches was otherwise unchanged though all showed substantial increases in approval.

(*b*) Legal abortion where the child may be deformed

The order in which the churches would approve the legalization of abortion in this situation was very little different from that for case (*a*) in 1966. The C. of E. and N.C. had approval rates above the national average, 'other religions' 5% below the average, C. of S. 13% below, those with no religion 25% below and R.C.s 27% below. The highest disapproval figures were among the no religion group 26%, and the R.C.s 36%. Those of no religion also produced a very high proportion of 'don't know' answers, 40%.

In 1967 the church categories were slightly different, 'the rest' subsuming 'other' and 'no religion', but allowing for this the order of the churches was unchanged. The C. of E. and N.C. approved most and disapproved least while the C. of S. and N.C. produced the only significant disapproval figures: 18% and 35% respectively. The extremities of the non-religious seem to have been cancelled out by the responses of the 'other religion' group with which they are here combined.

(c) *Legal abortion where the family does not have enough money to support another child*

In the 1966 survey the churches fall into a slightly different order of approval of abortion in case (c). Again the C. of E. and N.C. showed higher than average approval and lower than average disapproval but they were closely followed by the 'no religion' group which indeed had the lowest disapproval figure but also a strikingly high 'don't know' response which again reached 40%. This consistently high 'don't know' response, which is usually characteristic of lower status groups, combined with a relatively high approval of abortion on financial grounds might tempt one to guess that poverty was a more real problem to the non-religious respondents than to most others. Probably more significant, however, is the narrower range of opinion over the three cases which this group displays and the very large indifferent or undecided contingent within it. One does not feel that on the whole this group was seared by either enthusiasm or moral indignation over this or any other issue. 'Other religions' and the C. of S. both showed below average approval and R.C. lowest of all, 20% (less than half the approval of R.C.s for clerical celibacy). All churches had higher 'don't know' figures than for cases (a) and (b).

In 1967 the positions were slightly altered. The highest approval figure was among 'the rest', followed by N.C. and only then by the C. of E., though the differences were slight and approval, in all three cases, was above the general average. 'The rest' also showed the lowest disapproval figure followed closely by the C. of E. and N.C. The C. of S. and more markedly the R.C.s again had high disapproval and low approval figures.

Other Variables

The 1966 survey related opinion to *size of household* and *age of children*. In cases (a) and (b) there was higher approval and lower disapproval the lower the age of the children. The lowest approval and highest disapproval came from households of 1 or 2, some of whom would be old people and many of whom would be the unmarried or childless couples. The response by family size varied from case to case. Perhaps the most interesting figure is the very low approval and high disapproval of legalizing abortion in cases of inadequate income in households of 7+, precisely those for whom the problem will often have had personal relevance. One is never sure, of course, how far family size is a function of class and religious identification, and it is as well to recall that working-class R.C.s were more inclined than their middle-class counterparts to accept the authority of the church without question.

The breakdown of opinion by *social class* shows very clearly in 1966 and less markedly in 1967 a higher approval and lower disapproval with higher social class. The difference between the two surveys is probably due to the use of different criteria for allocating respondents to the various class categories. It is particularly interesting to note that the class difference showed more clearly when this was predominantly an income rather than an occupational status criterion. In particular the 'Very Poor' in 1966 were markedly more illiberal than the other income groups which were bunched fairly closely together. Except in case (*c*) which remains paradoxical this renders more plausible the previous speculation about the generally low-class position of the 'No religion' group.

The results analysed by *age* were strikingly consistent in both surveys despite the fact that slightly different age ranges were involved. Highest approval and lowest disapproval came in the second youngest group, 25–34 in 1966 and 30–44 in 1967. In both cases this is probably the group most involved in immediate family planning decisions. Approval decreased and disapproval increased with each increase in age, the youngest group coming midway between extremes. The only divergence from this pattern came in case (*c*) in the later survey where highest approval was shared by the 16–29 and 45–64 groups.

Differences of opinion by sex in 1966 showed women approving more often and disapproving less often than men of legal abortion on all three grounds. In 1967, however, there is no clear or consistent sex difference – male opinion seems to have moved more than female opinion over the period.

The special survey of R.C.s of March 1967 also contained a question (No. 10) on abortion. In case (*a*), where the health of the mother is in danger, Catholic approval is greater and disapproval less than that of the R.C. sub-sample in the general surveys, perhaps indicating that the trend to greater tolerance of abortion in this situation was a continuing one. In case (*b*), where the child may be deformed, R.C. opinion seems to have been more nearly stationary. The third sub-section of the question in the survey of R.C.s concerned abortion 'where the mother wants it'. This is not strictly comparable with case (*c*) in the general surveys. Only 11% approved and as many as 73% disapproved here. In all cases those who went to Mass frequently approved less and disapproved more than those who were lapsed or irregular attenders. However, against what the general surveys make likely, the lower classes approved more and in most instances disapproved less than the upper classes. The reason for this apparent contradiction would surely be worth exploration by further research. It may be related to an over-representation of the lower classes among the irregular church-goers. But this probably holds for all churches and so does not solve the problem. Does it perhaps mean that residual adherents of some other churches are less rather than more in favour of the legalization of abortion than are the regular church-goers? Does it suggest a different pattern of opinion by social class for different churches?

The findings for opinion by sex strengthen the suspicion that the R.C. pattern of opinion on abortion may be different from that of some other churches and of the general average. In the special survey of R.C.s, women (the more institutionally involved) approved less and disapproved more in all cases than did men (the less institutionally involved). It is plausible to suppose that regularity of attendance and greater willingness to accept the church's authority explain the relatively greater disapproval of abortion by R.C. women.

The questions on contraception (Nos. 7, 8 and 9) might be usefully noted here since they also concern the issue of family limitation. There was relatively greater feeling that there could be good reasons for the use of contraception in marriage (66%) and that the Pope should approve the use of the Pill for health reasons (70%), than there was tolerance of abortion, though only 38% felt that anyone who wanted should be permitted to use the Pill. Women approved contraception slightly more than men – the reverse of opinion on abortion – and here the connection between involvement in the church and disagreement with authority's ruling moves in an unexpected direction. It is, of course, easy to see why the child-bearing sex should prefer contraception to abortion, and women's normal conservatism may in addition be partly offset on this issue by the awareness that the hierarchy is seriously contemplating a change of teaching on contraception.

Opinion analysed by social class has some curious features. Substantially more upper than lower class respondents felt that

G

there could be good reasons for the use of contraception in marriage, yet opinions on the desirability of the Pill showed no class differences. Those of the lower classes who felt the use of the Pill for health reasons should be approved number 7% more than the proportion who had thought there could ever be good reasons for the use of contraception in marriage. There is perhaps some discontinuity between the concept 'contraception' and 'the Pill' among this group. Women showed a similar strong contradiction over this.

(4) *Divorce*

The special survey of R.C.s and a general survey undertaken in May 1965 explored opinion on divorce.

In the general survey the following opinions were discovered (see Tables 8a and 8b):

(*a*) 42% of respondents agreed with the suggestion that there should be no divorce between parents of children under 16 years;
36% disagreed;
22% did not know what to think.

(*b*) 53% supported the suggestion that where there are no children under the age of 16 the husband and wife should be able to get a divorce if they both agree they want one;
24% opposed this;
23% did not know what to think.

These were very specific questions and did not in themselves measure approval of divorce by consent in all cases, nor of total disapproval of divorce. The reasoning behind these figures is obscure and probably very varied. Perhaps the most significant figure is the 'don't know' response which reaches almost a quarter in both questions. The range of opinion between the churches is relatively slight. The C. of E. and N.C. returned almost identical responses on both questions. In response to question (*a*) they approved the suggestion only slightly more than they disapproved it, while in response to question (*b*) they approved the suggestion more than twice as strongly as they disapproved it. The 24% C. of E. and 26% N.C. disapproval of divorce by consent where there are no children under 16 is probably little more than the percentage in these churches who totally disapprove divorce. The C. of S. returned the highest 'don't know' figure – over a third in both questions – while as one might expect, R.C.s approved the first suggestion more and the second less than the other churches, though even so only 52% approved no divorce in case (*a*) and only 32% disapproved divorce by consent in case (*b*).

Men approved the first suggestion more than women who returned 'don't know' answers. Support for the second suggestion was almost equally divided between the sexes, but men opposed divorce by consent in case (*b*) 10% more often than women who again returned more 'don't know' answers. This figure perhaps hints that one should not take too seriously the popular argument that divorce by consent would involve erring husbands coercing unwilling wives into agreeing to a divorce.

There was unfortunately no analysis by social class or age.

Question 11 of the special survey of R.C.s produced a Catholic response different from that in the general surveys, although the phrasing of the questions was not identical and therefore comparison is risky. In the survey of R.C.s 30% believed that divorce should be not allowed in any circumstances, and a further 16% thought that it should be made more difficult, while 22% wanted it left as it is and 24% wanted it made easier. The first two groups together produce considerably more than the 32% who disapproved of divorce by consent where there were no children under 16. The irregular church-goers favoured easier divorce more than did the regular church-goers, men more than women and the lower than the upper social classes. Again it is hardly surprising to find religious commitment linked with conservative views on an issue which the Catholic church regards very seriously.

The next questions impinge more on the political sphere. Family law, of which abortion and divorce law are parts, tends to be treated as an issue of conscience rather than an issue of party politics, whereas attitudes to the questions which follow come closer to ideological and party orientations.

(5) *Road Safety* (see Table 9)

Two questions on road safety were included in a survey undertaken from December 1965 to early January 1966, immediately after the Christmas and New Year accident peak. The Labour Government had proposed the first rule and experimentally introduced the second as part of an attempt to reduce motor accidents. Neither question was analysed with reference to age or social class.

(*a*) 59% of respondents approved the Government's suggestion that random breathalyser tests should be introduced;
27% disapproved;
15% did not know what to think.

The most unexpected figure is the slightly below average approval of both N.C. and the C. of S., the latter in addition having the highest disapproval. This hardly confirms the stereotype of the Protestant brandishing his teetotal pledge. It could, of course, be no measure of the strength of Protestant disapproval of alcohol, but it may reflect a laissez-faire individualism which still opposes state interference with the freedom of the individual. In the C. of S. it may even have been due to a sense of outrage at interference with the Scots' New Year celebrations. 'The rest' produced low approval and high 'don't know' figures in comparison with the churches. The highest approval came from R.C.s. Differences however were very slight.

(*b*) 69% of the respondents approved the introduction of a 70 m.p.h. speed limit;
19% thought it a bad thing;
12% did not know what to think.

Again the range of opinion among the churches was very narrow. R.C.s approved most, the C. of S. disapproved most and 'the rest' approved least. As in the previous question N.C. and C. of E. were close to the average pattern of response, though N.C. produced the lowest disapproval figure. One again suspects laissez-faire individualism in the C. of S. There may be a slight dominance of pedestrian perspective among R.C.s who are generally of lower status and income than the other churches and therefore may contain proportionately fewer car drivers. Perhaps more important, however, is the fact confirmed by question 11 of the special survey of R.C.s that the party with the greatest support in this church is the Labour Party which as the Government was responsible for both these road safety suggestions.

(6) *The Colour Question*

A number of surveys and questions impinge on this issue, some of which are obviously in the political rather than the social/moral category. All should be taken as part of a continuous complex of opinion.

Relations between White and Coloured in Britain

In November 1965 a survey was carried out which contained three questions on the colour problem in Britain. Unfortunately, figures are only available for opinions by church and not by sex, age, social class or colour (see Table 10).

(a) 18% felt that relations between white and coloured persons in this country were getting better;
38% felt they were getting worse;
31% that they were remaining the same;
14% did not know what to think.

The C. of E., C. of S. and R.C. roughly in that order, were most pessimistic about relations between white and coloured people, while 'the rest', who would be likely to contain more coloured people than most of the churches, were more optimistic and N.C. put the most favourable interpretation on white/coloured relations. This probably partly reflects the general moral optimism of the English Protestant tradition but may also reflect the success with which some N.C. congregations, especially in Methodism, have absorbed coloured people, usually middle class Africans; West Indians, however, have tended either to lapse from the parent body of their mission church or to form their own churches on more evangelical, even sectarian lines.

(b) 17% of respondents felt more favourable towards coloured people (but than when?);
15% felt less favourable;
58% felt much the same;
9% did not know what to think.

'The rest' admitted more changes of attitude in both directions than did any of the churches. N.C. reported little improvement and little deterioration and 77% boasted consistency as compared with an average figure of 58%. R.C.s reported most improvement and least deterioration of attitude among the churches.

(c) 11% of respondents said there was a colour problem in their district;
81% said that there was not;
8% did not know what to think.

This is probably the most revealing question of all. Only R.C.s and 'the rest' had any sizeable proportion who thought there was a colour problem in their area, the two groups most likely to contain substantial lower-working-class proportions. This is probably a crude but not insignificant indication of the relative contact of the churches with coloured people, or rather with low-status coloured people. It is, therefore, very interesting to find that among R.C.s contact with the colour problem seems to go alongside the development of more favourable attitudes to coloured people, in 'the rest' it accompanies the development of both favourable and unfavourable attitudes. But these figures conceal more than they reveal. In what circumstances – including the participants' religious identification, moral attitudes, class, colour, sex, etc. – does personal contact with coloured people lead to more favourable or to less favourable attitudes to them? These figures hint that contact itself may produce changes of attitude, but one cannot even guess at the factors which influence the direction of the changes.

IV   Political Questions

The next questions have a clearly political focus though the colour question recurs.

(1) *Voting Behaviour*

In a survey dated September 1965 a question was asked about voting behaviour if the candidate of the party which the respondent normally supported happened to be a member of a particular out-group (see Table 11).

84% said they would vote for a R.C.;
78% for a woman;
76% for a Jew;
58% for an atheist;
58% for a coloured person.

This shows a very interesting scale of descending approval.

It is a great pity that the churches were divided only into C. of E., R.C., 'other' and 'none'. The most interesting single finding is the extremely illiberal pattern of opinion in the 'no religion' group. They approved candidates from all these out-groups except the atheist less than any of the churches. The R.C.s were most liberal in the case of women, Jews and R.C.s. The only real out-group to Catholics were atheists.

The least liberal age group was 65+ followed rather surprisingly by the youngest group, 16–24. The 25–34 group was almost always most liberal followed by the 35–44 and less closely by the 45–64 groups.

Sex differences on R.C.s, Jews and coloured persons were insignificant but men are more in favour of atheists and women of women.

The higher classes were consistently more tolerant than all the lower classes, a fact which makes R.C. liberality the more striking. The political complexion of Catholicism, its Socialist bias, may outweigh the effect of, as well as stem from, its class composition. It is a great pity that the political allegiance of the other churches is not documented here.

(2) *Rhodesia*

In October 1965 and again in December 1965 and January 1966, surveys sounded opinion on Rhodesian U.D.I. and its consequences (see Tables 12 and 13). It is impossible to comment usefully on these figures since the meaning of the questions is open to a great variety of interpretation and the reasoning behind responses is more obscure than usual. The figures are simply presented for the interpretation of the reader, with only three broad comments. First, R.C.s supported the Labour Government's handling of the Rhodesian issue more strongly than other churches. Second, the combination in the C. of S. of disapproval of government policy with highly egalitarian ideals for white/coloured relations in Rhodesia is noteworthy. Both reactions probably relate to the special involvement of Scottish Presbyterians with this part of Africa to which they have contributed significant numbers of migrants. The third point of interest is the very surprising lack of support from N.C. for the ideal of equal political and social development for black and white populations in Rhodesia and South Africa. This is entirely inconsistent with other N.C. reactions in this collection of surveys and with N.C. responses on similar questions elsewhere.[3]

In conclusion one can do little more than restate the need for a systematic, and probably extensive, exploration of some of the hypotheses which these figures suggest. What is needed is a delineation of the opinions of the churches when they are matched for all the important variables discussed here. Only then could one have any reliable guide to the influence of religion on opinions and attitudes in Britain.

NOTES

1. See, for example, D. A. Martin, *A Sociology of English Religion*, London: SCM Press, 1967: B. Wilson, *Religion in Secular Society*, London: Watts, 1966.

2. See H. Carrier, *The Psychology of Religious Belonging*, New York: Herder, 1965; London: Darton, Longman and Todd, 1966.

3. See, for example, ABC Television publication, *Television and Religion*, London: University of London Press, 1965.

TABLES

Table 1　THEOLOGICAL BELIEFS

(a) Which of these statements comes closest to your belief?

	TOTAL	Religion					Occupation				Age				Sex	
							Manual		Non-manual							
		C of E	NC	C of S	RC	Rest	Skilled	Other	Prof. man.	Other	16–29	30–44	45–64	65+	Men	Women
There is a personal god	38	34	33	57	66	28	33	37	47	39	34	35	41	46	30	45
There is some sort of spirit/god or life force	33	37	40	23	24	24	34	29	32	39	31	33	37	24	33	33
I don't know what to think	20	22	18	13	10	25	21	23	16	16	24	19	17	22	22	18
Don't really think there is any sort of spirit/ god or life force	9	7	9	7	—	23	12	11	5	6	11	12	5	8	15	4

Dates of fieldwork: 29 March–4 April 1963

(b) Do you believe that Jesus Christ was the Son of God or just a man?

	TOTAL	C of E	NC	C of S	RC	Rest	Skilled	Other	Prof. man.	Other	16–29	30–44	45–64	65+	Men	Women
Son of God	59	61	64	70	85	29	58	55	63	64	54	58	62	64	46	71
Just a man	17	17	17	10	6	26	18	15	16	19	19	16	16	15	20	13
Just a story	8	4	5	12	1	26	8	9	8	5	6	11	6	7	11	5
Don't know	16	18	14	8	8	19	16	21	13	12	21	15	16	14	23	11

Dates of fieldwork: 29 March–4 April 1963

Table 1 THEOLOGICAL BELIEFS—*continued*

(c) Do you believe there is or is not a life after death?

| | TOTAL | Religion | | | | | Occupation | | | | Age | | | | Sex | |
		C of E	NC	C of S	RC	Rest	Manual Skilled	Other	Non-manual Prof. man.	Other	16–29	30–44	45–64	65+	Men	Women
Is life after death	53	52	51	74	75	32	50	46	64	58	44	51	60	55	45	59
Is not	22	22	17	16	12	36	24	24	18	20	28	24	16	24	26	19
Don't know	25	26	32	10	12	32	26	30	18	22	28	25	24	21	29	22

Dates of fieldwork: 29 March–4 April 1963

(d) Do you believe that there is or is not a devil?

| | TOTAL | Religion | | | | | Occupation | | | | Age | | | | Sex | |
		C of E	NC	C of S	RC	Rest	Manual Skilled	Other	Non-manual Prof. man.	Other	16–29	30–44	45–64	65+	Men	Women
Is	36	32	38	54	61	26	33	32	42	43	36	34	36	40	32	39
Is not	46	49	39	37	29	57	46	46	50	45	46	52	43	43	50	44
Don't know	18	19	23	9	10	17	21	22	8	12	18	14	21	17	18	17

Dates of fieldwork: 29 March–April 4 1963

Table 2 ECUMENICAL NEGOTIATIONS

(a) Would you approve or disapprove if there were negotiations between all the churches – Roman Catholic, Greek Orthodox, Church of England and all the other churches in the world – on the question of all of them uniting?

(b) If there were any negotiations, do you think they would be likely to be successful or not?

	TOTAL	C of E	NC	C of S	RC	Other	None	Men	Women
(a) Approve	60	63	65	54	63	49	38	60	60
Disapprove	25	22	17	33	25	32	24	27	23
Don't know	15	15	18	13	12	19	38	13	17
(b) Likely to be successful	26	25	27	26	27	24	21	27	24
Not likely	57	58	57	61	58	50	52	58	56
Don't know	17	17	16	13	15	26	27	15	20

Dates of fieldwork: 29 September–6 October 1962

Table 3 ECUMENICAL NEGOTIATIONS

(a) Would you approve or disapprove if there were negotiations between the Church of England and the Non-conformist churches on the question of all of them uniting?

(b) Would you approve or disapprove if similar negotiations took place between the Roman Catholic Church and all other churches in this country?

| | TOTAL | Religion | | | | | Occupation | | | | Age | | | | Sex | |
		C of E	NC	C of S	RC	Rest	Manual Skilled	Other	Non-manual Prof.	Other man.	16-29	30-44	45-64	65+	Men	Women
(a) Negotiations between Church of England and Non-conformist																
Approve	59	64	58	46	59	39	49	58	65	64	54	58	63	60	52	65
Disapprove	14	11	16	32	17	12	20	13	13	12	14	13	13	18	15	13
Don't mind	18	17	18	14	20	21	21	19	12	17	19	22	15	15	20	16
Don't know	9	7	8	8	4	27	9	10	10	7	13	7	9	7	13	6
(b) Negotiations between Roman Catholic and other churches																
Approve	48	52	41	39	62	33	43	47	49	55	48	53	49	41	46	51
Disapprove	26	25	33	44	24	14	31	24	30	24	25	22	27	34	25	27
Don't mind	15	15	13	11	11	25	19	16	13	13	16	17	14	13	16	14
Don't know	10	8	13	6	3	28	7	13	8	9	12	8	10	12	13	7

Dates of fieldwork: 23–29 January 1967

Table 4   INFLUENCE OF RELIGION

(a) At the present time, do you think religion as a whole is increasing its influence on British life or decreasing its influence?

	TOTAL	Religion					Sex	
		C of E	NC	C of S	RC	Rest	Men	Women
Increasing	11	11	11	11	15	7	10	11
Same	20	22	27	21	10	16	22	19
Decreasing	55	55	53	47	54	62	57	53
Don't know	14	12	9	11	21	15	11	17

Dates of fieldwork: 6–11 May 1965

(b) At the present time, do you think religion as a whole is increasing its influence on British life or losing its influence?

	TOTAL	Religion				Other None		Class		Age			Sex	
		C of E	NC	C of S	RC	Other	None	Upper	Lower	16–34	35–44	45+	Men	Women
Increasing	9	6	10	12	18	14	6	8	9	8	13	7	7	10
No change	19	18	23	16	22	13	15	18	19	20	16	19	17	20
Losing influence	65	69	59	60	55	63	58	69	62	64	63	65	68	61
Don't know	8	6	8	12	5	10	21	4	10	8	8	9	7	9

Dates of fieldwork: 2–7 May 1967

Table 5 STANDARDS OF PUBLIC BEHAVIOUR

In general, are you satisfied or dissatisfied with standards of public behaviour?

	TOTAL	Religion					Occupation				Age				Sex	
							Manual		Non-manual							
		C of E	NC	C of S	RC	Rest	Skilled	Other	Prof. man.	Other	16-29	30-44	45-64	65+	Men	Women
Satisfied	43	43	36	37	51	43	47	40	44	42	52	50	37	25	52	34
Dissatisfied	46	44	56	57	38	46	42	44	49	48	31	40	52	64	39	52
Don't know	11	13	8	6	11	11	11	16	7	10	17	10	11	11	9	14

Dates of fieldwork: 29 March–4 April 1963

Table 6 ABORTION OPERATIONS

(i) Do you think abortion operations should or should not be legal in the following cases?

| | | Region | | | | Class | | | | Age | | | | | Sex | |
	TOTAL	South	Mid-lands/Wales	North	Scot-land	U.S. Jan. 1966	Av.+	Av.	Av.–	Very poor	16-24	25-34	35-44	45-64	65+	Men	Women
(a) Where the health of the mother is in danger?																	
Should	79	87	71	82	71	77	86	84	81	60	79	90	82	80	64	74	85
Should not	9	5	10	9	18	16	2	5	8	24	7	4	8	9	17	11	6
Don't know	12	8	18	9	12	7	12	11	11	16	14	6	9	11	19	14	9
(b) Where the child may be born deformed?																	
Should	71	78	63	74	58	54	84	73	72	54	71	77	72	73	58	65	76
Should not	13	9	13	12	26	32	5	12	12	22	13	8	12	12	18	15	10
Don't know	16	12	23	15	16	14	12	15	16	24	16	15	15	15	24	19	14
(c) Where the family does not have enough money to support another child?																	
Should	33	35	27	40	28	18	35	34	35	23	26	40	38	34	25	29	37
Should not	43	45	41	39	49	72	40	44	41	50	52	37	42	42	43	45	40
Don't know	24	20	32	21	23	10	26	22	24	27	22	22	20	25	32	25	23

Dates of fieldwork: 11-15 February 1966

Table 6 ABORTION OPERATIONS—*continued*

(ii) Do you think abortion operations should or should not be legal in the following cases?

	TOTAL	Religion						Number in household				Age of children			
		C of E	NC	C of S	RC	Other	None	1 or 2	3 or 4	5 or 6	7+	0-4	5-10	11-15	16-20
(a) Where the health of the mother is in danger?															
Should	79	87	78	70	57	75	57	79	81	77	79	89	84	76	73
Should not	9	5	5	16	28	7	11	10	7	9	10	6	8	9	9
Don't know	12	8	17	14	15	17	33	10	12	14	11	5	8	15	18
(b) Where the child may be born deformed?															
Should	71	79	73	58	43	66	46	66	75	70	77	80	75	70	69
Should not	13	8	9	26	36	9	14	15	11	11	12	8	10	11	14
Don't know	16	13	18	16	20	26	40	19	14	19	11	12	15	18	17
(c) Where the family does not have enough money to support another child?															
Should	33	38	38	22	15	25	34	29	36	35	28	33	42	34	33
Should not	43	40	36	59	61	44	26	45	42	38	50	46	37	36	41
Don't know	24	22	27	20	25	32	40	25	22	26	22	21	22	30	26

Dates of fieldwork: 11–15 February 1966

Table 7 ABORTION OPERATIONS—continued

Do you think abortion operations should or should not be legal in the following cases?

	TOTAL	Religion					Occupation				Age				Sex	
							Manual		Non-manual							
		C of E	NC	C of S	RC	Rest	Skilled	Other	Prof.	Other man.	16-29	30-44	45-64	65+	Men	Women
(a) Where the health of the mother is in danger?																
Should be legal	86	90	88	95	64	82	89	83	89	89	87	90	85	79	86	86
Should not	7	5	4	3	24	5	3	9	4	6	4	6	8	9	6	8
Don't know	7	6	8	2	12	13	9	8	6	4	9	3	7	11	+8	6
(b) Where the child may be born deformed?																
Should be legal	76	82	78	75	49	73	81	73	79	79	77	84	73	69	77	76
Should not	13	9	9	18	35	10	9	14	9	14	12	10	15	14	11	14
Don't know	11	9	12	7	16	18	10	13	12	8	11	6	12	18	12	10
(c) Where the family does not have enough money to support another child?																
Should be legal	37	38	41	30	20	48	36	34	37	42	39	36	39	31	35	39
Should not	46	44	40	60	61	33	43	48	46	42	42	54	42	43	48	44
Don't know	17	18	19	10	19	19	21	18	17	15	19	10	19	27	18	17

Dates of fieldwork: 23–29 January 1967

Table 8 DIVORCE

(a) A judge has suggested that there should be no divorce between parents of children under 16 years of age. Do you agree or disagree with this suggestion?

	TOTAL	Religion					Sex	
		C of E	NC	C of S	R C	Rest	Men	Women
Agree	42	42	43	40	52	35	45	40
Disagree	36	38	38	24	25	38	38	34
Don't know	22	20	19	36	23	27	17	26

Dates of fieldwork: 6–11 May 1965

(b) He also suggested that where there are no children under the age of 16, the husband and wife should be able to get a divorce if they both agree they want one. Would you support or oppose such a change in the law?

	TOTAL	Religion					Sex	
		C of E	NC	C of S	R C	Rest	Men	Women
Support	53	56	58	40	45	55	54	53
Oppose	24	24	26	25	32	18	30	20
Don't know	23	20	16	35	23	27	16	27

Dates of fieldwork: 6–11 May 1965

Table 9 ROAD SAFETY

(a) The Government is proposing to introduce breathalyser tests which will mean stopping motorists at random to check how much alcohol in their blood. Do you approve or disapprove of this proposal?

(b) Do you think it is a good thing or a bad thing that a 70 m.p.h. speed limit is being applied to all roads and motorways?

| | TOTAL | RELIGION | | | | |
		C of E	NC	C of S	RC	Rest
(a) Random breathalyser tests						
Approve	59	59	58	53	63	54
Disapprove	27	28	23	36	26	21
Don't know	15	13	19	10	11	25
(b) 70 m.p.h. speed limit						
Good thing	69	71	70	63	73	58
Bad thing	19	19	16	30	19	16
Don't know	12	11	14	6	8	26

Dates of fieldwork: 31 December 1965–4 January 1966

Table 10 COLOUR ISSUE

(a) Would you say that in this country the feeling between white people and coloured people is getting better, getting worse or remaining the same?

(b) What are your own feelings towards coloured people: more favourable, less favourable or the same?

(c) Do you think there is or is not a colour problem in the district where you live?

	TOTAL	C of E	NC	C of S	RC	Rest
				RELIGION		
(a) Relations between white/coloured people in this country						
Getting better	18	14	46	13	15	24
Getting worse	38	42	29	37	28	35
Remaining same	31	30	18	42	38	29
Don't know	14	15	7	9	19	13
(b) Own feelings towards coloured people						
More favourable	17	16	6	19	21	25
Less favourable	15	16	13	14	12	21
Same	58	58	77	66	54	47
Don't know	9	10	4	1	14	8
(c) Coloured problem in district where you live						
Is colour problem	11	9	5	1	21	21
Is not	81	82	93	98	71	64
Don't know	8	9	2	1	8	15

Dates of fieldwork: 4–9 November 1965

Table 11 VOTING BEHAVIOUR

(a) If the party of your choice nominated a generally well qualified person as a Parliamentary candidate and he happened to be a Roman Catholic, would you vote for him?

(b) Would you vote for him if he happened to be a Jew?

(c) What if he was coloured?

(d) A woman?

(e) Or an atheist?

Would vote for	TOTAL	Religion				Class		Age					Sex	
		C of E	RC	Other	None	Upper	Lower	16–24	25–34	35–44	45–64	65+	Men	Women
Roman Catholic	84	82	99	83	77	89	82	81	85	86	85	77	83	85
Jew	76	76	79	75	71	83	73	68	83	78	77	69	76	75
Coloured person	58	57	61	63	54	62	57	53	65	64	56	51	58	59
Woman	78	78	82	81	67	84	77	73	80	77	80	80	76	81
Atheist	58	57	53	55	78	67	55	59	66	64	54	46	65	50

Dates of fieldwork: 10–15 September 1965

Table 12   RHODESIA SITUATION

(a) Do you approve or disapprove of the Government's handling of the situation in Rhodesia?

(b) What do you think should be the attitude of Europeans in Rhodesia and South Africa towards the coloured native population?

	TOTAL	RELIGION				
		C of E	NC	C of S	RC	Rest
(a) Government handling						
Approve	36	40	31	28	46	20
Disapprove	23	17	42	31	17	28
Don't know	41	43	27	41	37	52
(b) Attitude of Europeans in Rhodesia/ South Africa to coloured native population						
Equal political rights and social equality	41	41	26	60	41	46
Equal political rights but separate social development	16	17	26	13	7	10
Both political/social development separate from Europeans	17	19	18	8	19	14
Don't know	26	24	30	19	34	30

Dates of fieldwork: 7–12 October 1965

Table 13 RHODESIA SITUATION

(a) Do you approve or disapprove of the Government's handling of the situation in Southern Rhodesia?

(b) Do you think the Government has been too strong in the action it has taken against Rhodesia, not strong enough or about right?

(c) Do you think that the Conservative Party should, or should not, support the Government's actions on Rhodesia?

(d) Do you think that Mr Smith will or will not succeed in his policy of seizing independence?

(e) Do you think that the situation in Rhodesia is or is not a threat to world peace?

			RELIGION			
	TOTAL	C of E	NC	C of S	RC	Rest
(a) Government's handling of Rhodesian situation						
Approve	51	49	58	33	65	49
Disapprove	26	28	17	27	19	23
Don't know	23	22	25	40	16	29
(b) Government action too strong	11	13	6	14	10	7
Not strong enough	30	33	23	21	17	37
About right	36	35	44	32	52	22
Don't know	23	20	27	33	21	34

Table 13 RHODESIA SITUATION—*continued*

	TOTAL	C of E	NC	RELIGION C of S	RC	Rest
(c) Conservative support for Government policy						
Should support	64	63	68	63	75	58
Should not	14	17	5	14	9	7
Don't know	22	20	27	23	15	35
(d) Success of Smith						
Will succeed	21	20	20	38	18	25
Will not	47	49	43	33	52	36
Don't know	32	31	38	29	30	39
(e) Rhodesia a threat to world peace						
Is threat	42	43	39	46	41	43
Is not	36	38	36	32	42	23
Don't know	21	19	25	22	18	34

Dates of fieldwork: 31 December 1965–4 January 1966

Table 14 GALLUP POLL WITH ROMAN CATHOLICS

Sample: 400 Roman Catholics, i.e. people who say 'Roman Catholic' in reply to the question 'What is your denomination'. Sample is representative of adult Roman Catholics, aged 16 and over in Great Britain. The sample was distributed over 37 points.

Fieldwork: 18–20 March 1967.

Definitions: 'Go to Mass—often' = at least 2 or 3 times a month. 'Go to Mass—rarely' = all others, including those who never go (14 per cent).

Question	Answer	Total	Go to Mass		Sex		Class	
			Often	Rarely	Men	Women	Upper	Lower
1. Do you accept the authority of the Roman Catholic Church without question or with some reservations?	Without question	53	58	39	46	58	45	55
	With some reservations	43	40	51	49	39	48	41
	Don't know	4	2	10	5	3	6	3
2. Do you think the Roman Catholic Church's authority over its members is too strict, not strict enough or about right?	Too strict	36	31	48	44	29	37	36
	Not strict enough	7	8	6	7	8	4	9
	About right	57	61	46	49	63	59	56
3. Do you think that laymen should or should not be allowed a greater share in the affairs of the Roman Catholic Church?	Should	50	50	50	53	48	58	47
	Should not	28	32	20	29	28	26	29
	Don't know	22	18	31	19	24	15	24
4. On the whole, do you think that Cardinal Heenan is doing a good job or a bad job as the leader of the Roman Catholic Church in Britain?	Good job	86	89	77	85	86	86	86
	Bad job	2	1	5	3	2	1	2
	Don't know	12	10	18	12	12	13	12
5. Do you think the relations of the Roman Catholic Church with other Christian Churches in Britain should be closer than they are at present or not?	Should be closer	81	78	87	83	79	83	80
	Should not	13	15	7	10	15	13	13
	Don't know	7	7	6	7	6	5	7
6. Do you think that all Christian denominations, including Roman Catholic, should take positive steps to unite in one church or would you be against such a move?	Should unite	56	53	65	60	53	68	51
	Against it	30	33	24	25	34	24	32
	Don't know	14	15	11	15	13	7	16

Table 14 GALLUP POLL WITH ROMAN CATHOLICS
—continued

Question	Answer	Total	Go to Mass		Sex		Class	
			Often	Rarely	Men	Women	Upper	Lower
7. Do you think that there could ever be good reasons for the use of contraceptive methods of birth control in marriage?	Good reasons	66	62	76	64	67	71	63
	No good reasons	24	28	14	23	25	23	25
	Don't know	10	10	10	13	8	6	12
8. Do you think that the Pope has taken too long in coming to a final decision on the contraceptive Pill or do you think that he is right in taking so long?	Too long	43	37	57	44	42	40	44
	Right	46	53	30	41	50	50	44
	Don't know	11	10	13	15	8	11	12
9. Do you think the Pope should or should not approve of the Pill:								
(a) When taken from health reasons?	Should approve	70	66	78	65	73	69	70
	Should not	13	13	12	12	14	10	14
	Don't know	17	21	9	23	12	21	16
(b) When taken by anyone who wants to take it?	Should approve	38	33	50	37	39	37	38
	Should not	43	48	32	39	47	41	44
	Don't know	19	19	18	24	14	22	17
10. Do you think abortion operations should or should not be legal in the following case:								
(a) Where the health of the mother is in danger?	Should be legal	69	64	81	73	65	66	70
	Should not	19	23	9	12	26	20	19
	Don't know	12	13	11	15	9	15	11
(b) Where the child may be born deformed?	Should be legal	47	39	68	51	44	37	51
	Should not	35	43	18	31	40	40	33
	Don't know	17	19	14	19	16	22	15
(c) Where the mother wants it?	Should be legal	11	6	21	15	7	5	13
	Should not	73	78	61	71	75	79	71
	Don't know	16	15	18	14	18	16	16
11. What is your attitude towards divorce, it should not be allowed at all, it should be easier than at present, it should be more difficult than at present?	Should not be allowed	30	36	16	26	33	29	30
	Should be easier	24	19	39	27	22	17	27
	Should be more difficult	16	16	16	17	15	15	16
	Leave as it is	22	22	22	20	24	29	19
	Don't know	8	8	7	10	6	10	7
12. Do you think that the present rules about marrying non-Catholics should be tightened up, made easier, abandoned altogether or left as they are?	Tightened up	7	7	5	6	7	8	6
	Easier	37	36	40	41	35	31	40
	Abandoned	17	13	25	22	12	24	14
	Left as they are	37	41	29	28	45	33	39
	Don't know	2	3	1	3	2	4	2

Table 14 GALLUP POLL WITH ROMAN CATHOLICS
—continued

Question	Answer	Total	Go to Mass		Sex		Class	
			Often	Rarely	Men	Women	Upper	Lower
13. Do you think that priests should be:	Encouraged to marry	5	5	4	6	4	6	4
	Permitted to marry	35	30	45	39	31	33	35
	Should hold to their vows of celibacy	44	48	33	37	49	44	44
	Don't know	17	17	18	19	16	17	17
14. Do you approve or disapprove of the use of English in the Mass in place of Latin?	Approve English	82	82	81	79	84	75	84
	Disapprove	13	13	15	14	12	17	12
	Don't know	5	5	4	6	4	8	4
15. From the point of view of the Church as a whole, do you think the other recent changes in the Mass are a good thing or not?	Good thing	65	69	55	63	67	65	65
	Not good	7	5	10	8	6	10	5
	Some good, some bad	14	16	8	11	16	12	14
	Don't know	14	10	26	18	11	14	15
16.								
(a) If there were a General Election tomorrow, which party would you support?	Conservative	29	31	25	31	28	42	24
	Labour	47	45	53	45	48	32	53
	Liberal	4	4	6	7	2	6	4
	Other	3	4	1	5	2	2	4
	Don't know	16	16	15	12	19	19	14
(b) *If don't know:* Which would you be most inclined to vote for?	Conservative	31	34	25	33	30	43	26
	Labour	52	49	57.	50	53	38	57
	Liberal	5	4	7	7	3	8	4
	Other	4	4	2	5	2	2	4
	Don't know	8	8	8	5	12	10	8
17. At present the Church insists that all Catholics must bring their children up as Catholics. Would you approve or disapprove if this rule were to be re-laxed in cases where a Catholic marries a non-Catholic?	Approve	41	36	52	39	42	29	46
	Disapprove	45	49	35	47	44	55	41
	Don't know	14	14	13	14	14	16	13
18. Should all elementary schools be taken over by local authorities or should the churches continue to manage some of them as they do now?	churches con-tinue	65	66	61	65	65	65	65
	Taken over	26	23	33	29	23	27	25
	Don't know	9	11	6	6	12	7	10

Table 14 GALLUP POLL WITH ROMAN CATHOLICS
—*continued*

Question	Answer	Total	Go to Mass		Sex		Class	
			Often	Rarely	Men	Women	Upper	Lower
19. How old were you when you finished your full-time education?	14 or under	44	43	46	47	40	18	54
	15	30	30	30	26	33	22	33
	16 or over	23	24	21	21	25	49	12
	University	4	4	4	6	2	12	0
20. Can you tell me your date of birth please?	16–34	39	40	44	40	40	44	39
	35–54	40	39	43	40	40	43	39
	55 and over	20	22	16	20	19	13	23
21. Sex	Man	48	45	54	100	0	46	48
	Woman – house-wife	39	40	36	0	74	38	40
	Woman – not housewife	13	15	10	0	26	16	12